Stonehenge Bluestone III

The Skull of Esus

Written by Neil A. Clark

Edited by Eric Franklin

Illustrated by Neil A. Clark
Eric Franklin & Mark Lepus

Special Pre-publication Limited Edition
for
Teachers and Students

© celtworld.co.uk

First published Spring Equinox, March 2012
as a limited edition hardback entitled:

"The Skull of Esus"

ISBN 9780955325762

Due Publication Date of this edition: 12. 12. 12.

Contents

Preface

Who are the Celts?

The ancient people around whose knowledge this book has been largely built emerge from prehistory in the Preseli Hills. They are often referred to within these pages as being of the Celtic Nation, but there is more than one view of who the Ancient Celts actually were. One of the more commonly accepted accounts is outlined in the book *Celtic Mythology* by Proinsias Mac Cana, who writes:

> By the fourth century BC the Celts were accounted one of the four peripheral nations of the known world, beside the Scythians, the Indians and the Ethiopians – and not without reason, for already they had begun to intrude themselves, rudely and dramatically, into the great Mediterranean centres of political and cultural influence. From their original homeland, which comprised southern Germany and part of Bohemia, they moved with explosive energy to the eastern and western limits of the European continent and threatened the rising power of Rome. By the end of the fifth century the area of Celtic settlement had already been extended beyond its original limits and in Spain Celtic peoples were well established over much of the country following successive immigrations.

These are the Celts of the classic view of history, but if you ask a Welshman with an interest in the past who the Preseli people were, he will say they, too, were of the Celtic Nation. If this is the case, how could the Celtic Nation have begun with a migration of people from Germany thousands of years after the Preseli people began to develop their civilisation? Who is right?

The people who, in this book, are considered the originators of an early British holistic socio-scientific philosophy, which I shall call 'Preseli Consciousness', were already established in Britain at a much earlier time than the Celts of Germany. Not only so, but they exercised a continuity of authority stretching from obscure, prehistoric antiquity right through to the Sixth Century, when Celtic Christianity was at its peak.

We must therefore regard these people as indigenous, and so to refer to them simplistically as 'Ancient Britons' would be misleading. There is much evidence to indicate that they were eventually part of a larger, theologically, if not politically, united nation, which, by the time of Stonehenge, extended across all of Western Britain, Ireland and down into France. This is the Celtic Nation referred to in this book, and these early British Celts, who were indeed of the stock of the Ancient Britons, developed their classic Celtic designs independently of, and long before, the German Migration referred to by Mac Cana.

To shine a brighter light on the question of identity it is helpful to go back even further, to the very beginnings of human presence in the north. The most commonly accepted view of the history of European Man is that Homo-Sapiens, or Cro-Magnon, migrated north out of Africa at around 30,000 BC and displaced the Neanderthals, who had previously thrived in the area now known as France.

In his book, *Footprints in the Stone*, however, David John Jones argues against this element of the conventional theory of human development and migration. The discoveries of the remains of 'Boxgrove Man', dated to 500,000 BC, and of 'The Red Man of Paviland' of 30,000 BC, in Southern Britain, clearly demonstrate that

6

modern humans were living in Britain long before the hitherto-accepted date of arrival of homo-sapiens in the north. Jones enlightens us thus:

> Boxgrove and Red Man provisionally dated from around 500,000 and 30,000 BC and thereafter, had actually evolved in the area of Britain in front of Neanderthal or the said "modern-humans" coming out of Africa at 30,000 BC. The early British resided northwest below the ice-shelf and quite apparently would have moved west and east and also back into the south from this latitude and this very location. It is the Boxgrove and Red Man's people who are the only candidates to be the very early British.

These people were the early ancestors of the Britons of today, who lived in Britain and ventured out to populate other lands, and mix with other races, over a considerable period of time. They pre-date any other modern Northern European counterparts, as only Neanderthals existed in that area until about 30,000 BC. These people, who have occupied their land since the earliest times, and whose descendants we know as the Ancient Celts, were the ancestors of an entity we must acknowledge as a Celtic Nation. They went on to become the manufacturers of classic 'Celtic' wares that modern studies distinguish as being produced thousands of years before the German migration began.

In reading this book it must therefore be remembered that when the terms 'Ancient Celts' and 'Neolithic Celts' are used within its pages the reference is not to the Celts of the later classic historical view, but to an older nation, spawned in no small part by the people we already vaguely name the 'Ancient Britons'.

This does not mean that the classical view is wrong, but simply that it is referring to a different history. It must also be remembered that, while the Celtic Nation referred to in this book undoubtedly had a dominant gene pool, its culture, which bequeathed to us its wisdom in that most durable of stuff, solid rock, proves by those relics that it was in truth a spiritual nation rather than a jealously self-guarding ethnic nation. Indeed, in the opinion of this author, the holistic philosophy that is the subject of this book was not intended by its sages to remain exclusively a Celtic possession. As it developed, its concepts took on a universal aspect that motivated the wish that it be used for the benefit of all humanity, and much independent archaeological evidence will be called upon here to demonstrate that its scientific discoveries, measurement systems and engineering principles were freely gifted to other distant societies.

This book hopefully upholds that noble tradition.

Introduction

The hypothesis described in this book is the culminating work of several years of conscientious research to find again a certain grain of truth, the fundamental wisdom that led to the great leap in human consciousness of the Neolithic Celtic Nation. Their rudimentary but pioneering approach to understanding the status and purpose of life in our universe was clearly highly beneficial to the development of their society, and may therefore be a gem of awareness that we in this modern age need more than any other to recover at the present critical stage of our own existence.

It must be noted that this book does not attempt to provide a comprehensive account of the journey of rediscovery. To gain a fuller appreciation of the intuitively directed process of reconstruction attempted here, it might be advisable to read the several more analytical titles that have preceded this one. However, if the primary interest of the reader lies in consideration of the final distillate of philosophy, painstakingly deciphered from the evidences unearthed along the way, then reading this book without acquaintance with its predecessors will hopefully prove worthwhile.

That being said, this book has no shortage of archaeological revelations of its own. These new discoveries, made by judicious reconsideration of the marks of the Ancients that survive in the landscape of today, are no less groundbreaking than those of the works that go before it. Bluestone exhibits a magnificent starry pattern when it is cut open, yet the idea that Stonehenge should be reassessed by contemplation of how it would have looked to its builders, with the newly-quarried Bluestones appearing as a dramatic image of the night sky, was dismissed by the academic community when first raised by this author in 2000 (and later reiterated by the same author in his Stonehenge documentary of 2004). However, this empathy with the Celtic age has recently been embraced by influential figures in the archaeological community, and will presumably become, in time, an accepted wisdom of their academic world. While discoveries such as this, though simple in essence, actually require considerable time and patience to unearth, it is very easy for others to appropriate them later. How long will it be before the new ideas in this book begin to appear, without being credited to their real originators, in the mainstream works of others?

Many archaeologists seem to allow their heads to be turned by the magnificence of the monuments they study, for they abandon the most basic requirements of logic when making their assessments. One classic example of this circumstance is the commonly cited claim that, the Pyramids being by far the greatest technological achievement of the ancient world, it was the Egyptians who informed the Celts how to build large-scale stone monuments. As Stonehenge predates the Pyramids, this is quite clearly not the case. It was the application of this simple and logical observational process that led this author to the geographical source of the new wisdom of the ancient world, the Preseli Hills of Wales.

The Preseli Cradle

The area of the Preseli Hills was one of the most heavily monumented areas of Britain, until recent times. Most readers will probably know that this is where the Bluestones of Stonehenge came from, but how many could say why the Bluestones were taken on such an epic journey to Wiltshire? No one can claim absolute certainty regarding this question, but anyone who has read the little book that precedes this one, *Stonehenge Bluestone II*, will in all probability come down on the side of the debate that favours the cosmic pattern theory, as bearing some considerable significance to the purpose of Stonehenge.

As the monuments of Preseli preceded the building works of the Stonehenge area, it takes little reflection to deduce that the purveyors of the Bluestones also facilitated the dissemination of an advanced socio-theological, scientific model, which was to shape the more eastern community whose subsequent achievements we are so familiar with. William Blake recognised this evolution. He and his friend William Stukeley attributed the driving force behind the development of the grand new temple of Stonehenge to an existing intelligentsia of supreme integrity, who they believed were the Druids. In this view, the Druids were philosophers who brought about a shift, not only in what we would call scientific understanding, but also in human consciousness itself. This shift in consciousness was separated from the old Pagan myth-based religion by its quest for truth through rational contemplation of the visible universe, and resulted in huge advances in the disciplines of astronomy, mathematics and engineering, as evidenced by the existence of monuments like Stonehenge. Paganism continued to flourish in the east, but the new wisdom had gained much ground.

Whether this giant leap in the methodology of the human quest for truth was actually attributable to the Druids is a matter for academic debate. Historians generally claim that, although the Druids were known to be masters of such disciplines, they did not actually exist at the time that the leap took place, some claiming that they did not appear until three centuries or so prior to the arrival of Christianity. This opinion is largely based on the testimony of Julius Caesar, who has provided us with one of the earliest accounts of the Druid Sect.

However, the intellectual leap that informed the Druids, and us for that matter, had taken place some three thousand years earlier, or more. In consequence, the Druids were, at the very least, the

11

inheritors of the grand philosophy that inspired and empowered the builders of Stonehenge. They were, therefore, the inheritors of what we in this book are calling 'Preseli Consciousness'. Archaeological and historical records support the hypothesis that a holistic, spiritual and scientific consciousness has inhabited the Celtic heartlands continuously from the Neolithic period to the present day. Whether the forefathers of this enlightened approach to the unravelling of the mysteries of the universe were called the Druids, or had some other title, is a purely academic argument. But we, in their far future, are interested in what they thought and did, and why they did it.

If we were to use only written history to date the era of the Druids we would have to believe that they had a very short reign, but it is the written records, not the Druids themselves, which cover a short time-span, being largely the product of Julius Caesar's very brief contacts with Britain. If, on the other hand, we use archaeological discoveries such as the Lunulae, elaborate gold breastplates believed to have been worn by Druid priests during their communication rites with aged oaks, the date of the establishment of this practice is pushed back to around the time of the building of Stonehenge.

Here we discover a more likely truth. The argument that the Druids were essentially a primitive group, who performed strange rites in secluded oaken clearings, is actually contradicted by the very same evidence that is used to make the case. While the Druids may have conducted rituals in the woods, it is also written that they were a highly educated people, who spoke several languages and were skilled in metallurgy, medicine, astronomy and many other disciplines. That the political elite of the era of Caesar chose to send their children to be educated in Druidic centres of learning suggests that the day to day dealings of the Druids were not conducted in secret or remote woodland locations at all The picture conjured by most historians is therefore seriously inaccurate. And, we may add, this is unsurprising since it is the intellectual tradition of the Roman empire, not that of the Druids, which has moulded the thought of today's academics.

Stukley and Blake were not of this mould. They felt that the lost knowledge of their ancestors would re-emerge at some point in the future, and the lost social archetype would consequently be restored, resulting in the salvation of humanity. Blake believed that the cradle of the Druids' rational monotheistic philosophy, 'the true Jerusalem', lay somewhere on British soil, founded in a time before the construction of Stonehenge, before the advent of Buddhist and Hindu philosophy, and even prior to the development of Chinese creationist thinking. Stukeley's imagination was primarily fed by archaeological observations while Blake derived his motivations from intuition, or 'channelling' as it would probably be labelled today.

Although Blake was convinced that 'Jerusalem' had existed in Britain and would emerge once more, he appeared to have no real idea of its actual geographic location. Today we know where that place is. It is the source of the Bluestones, the Preseli Hills of South West Wales, the former domain of the pioneering Britons and the cradle of that monotheist holistic philosophy, now dubbed 'Preseli Consciousness' by those of us who have joined the revivalist movement. This place is more commonly referred to as 'The Preseli Complex', but we shall afford it the more fitting title of 'The Preseli Cradle'. In his book *The New View over Atlantis* John Michell comments on Blake's vision as follows:

Nothing less than the recreation of the old system of spiritual engineering whose ruins are still visible in every corner of the country. From the rocks, mountains and headlands a mysterious current once flowed down avenues of standing stones over mounds and earthworks towards some central hill dedicated to Mercury, the terrestrial spirit. Below the hill an instrument of solar generation produced the spark by which the current became animated and recoiled in a wave of fertility through the hidden veins of the land.

Those familiar with the circle of Gors Fawr and the Carn Meini outcrop in the Preseli Hills, (the source of the Stonehenge

13

Bluestones) will surely wonder at the remarkable resemblance of Michell's description to that particular site. If you follow what is perhaps the most important ley line in the world, starting from Mecca, you will pass directly over the Pyramids of Egypt and on through the centre of Stonehenge, arriving inexorably at the scattered remains of an avenue of once-magnificent standing stones. These stones, which originally formed a dramatic gateway to the Preseli Cradle, are now, sadly, gone. They were smashed in relatively recent times to clear the way for agriculture.

The Skull of Esus within the Circle of the Keepers of Truth

But, by great fortune, two contemporary New Age icons of Preseli Consciousness, the Skull of Esus and the Circle of the Keepers of Truth, have been carved from the sacred remnants of two of the most highly patterned of these lost stones.

Who is Seus?

Seus is an anagrammatic expression of the name Esus, also known as Hesus, who was a Celtic deity or shaman about whom very little is known. Seus features as the protagonist of the book *The Tome of Seus*, which provided the primary inspiration for the holistic, philosophical concepts developed within this title. There are two

14

stone carvings of Esus in France, which depict him as a woodsman, and stories of Esus being the awaited messiah of the Celts remain in circulation to this day. *The Tome of Seus*, rightly or wrongly, provides a greater picture, implying that Esus was a Celt who achieved enlightenment at Carn Meini, and then gifted his wisdom to the 'Keepers of Truth', an elite sect within the Druids, to be used for the benefit of humanity. When he died he promised his king that he would return one day, as the son of a then-future Celtic King, and requested that his king instruct his people to build a Bluestone temple on the Wiltshire Downs.

The reader may be interested to learn that the notion that Stonehenge was built in Bluestone from the outset, with no temporary or first-stage period as a henge of wood, and that it was used as a monument to 'enlightened ancestors', was first revealed when *The Tome of Seus* was published in 2008. The elimination of the postulated 'Woodhenge' period is highly significant, for it pushed the construction of Stonehenge back by about 500 years, a dating that was later positively confirmed in a BBC documentary of 2009 by well-known British professional archaeologists Wainwright and Darvill.

In *The Tome of Seus*, the concept of the returning shaman Esus also relates to the 'Triune God' of Christianity, with Esus reincarnating as Jesus at the appropriate moment in history. The book also predicts a third and final incarnation, and this subject will be discussed in greater detail in due course.

Considerable historical evidence to support this unorthodox scenario actually exists, some of it in the *New Testament*, its deeper significance unnoticed by readers who have not the necessary familiarity with the differences between competing Christian doctrines concerning the Kingdom of God. This matter will not be debated here, but those interested in learning more about the connection between Jesus, the Celtic Royals and the Druids should read the book by Einon Johns, *The Almighty King*.

The Structure of the Tome

Recommended Reading: *The Tome of Seus - A Brief Homage* – from *The Depth of Evil*, pages 5-7, transcribed below.

The Tome of Seus is divided into eight threads, some of which have completely independent timelines. For example, the religious allegory spans the years from the time of Jesus to the present day, while the political timeline covers a period of just sixty-four years. This can make the book difficult to understand at times, but it may be helpful to note that all the timelines encoded within the text eventually converge at a precise and infamous date, the eleventh of September 2001.

This text primarily refers to the political allegories, but also negotiates the technological thread, referred to as *The Practice*, which is inextricably connected via the same timeline. The political history is divided into two threads, called *The Tyranny* and *The Toil*. The first relates to the conspiracies of an alleged secret coalition of the political, industrial and military elite of America.

The second refers to the history of the era from the perspective of the people who quietly risked all, in a struggle to free their world from the grip of its tyrannical oppressors. Both threads have their feet firmly planted in the real history of our times, but very few of the foot soldiers of the struggle for freedom are actually named in the text. In contrast, the perpetrators of *The Tyranny* are almost always identified, mainly through the use of anagrams.

Some of the characters are personifications of institutions, or equate to a progression of closely associated people from the real world. One such example of this is Cester Vicrees, whose name is an anagram of Secret Service. He is initially introduced as 'Head of the Closet Facility', representing the US Military's wartime Secret Services, but his character goes on to become head of the

'Independent Closet Authority' or 'ICA'. As such he is representative of a number of individuals, primarily the wartime agent and chief player in the formation of the Central Intelligence Agency, Allan Dulles, and ultimately becomes an embodiment of the CIA organization as a whole.

In short, the political allegory of *The Tome of Seus* is revealed as a US-focused equivalent of the anti-Soviet propaganda publication, *Animal Farm*, albeit in a more specific and detailed form. As such, this seemingly innocent tale of a parallel world turns the tables on the Western Establishment by exposing the perpetrators of Democracy as corrupt and greedy oppressors, who collude to mercilessly exploit the populace of the globe through the use of deception and aggression.

Note: For those who are interested in the politics of *The Tome of Seus*, there is a very comprehensive glossary at the back of *The Depth of Evil*, which provides all the necessary information to decipher and digest the relevant allegories.

So now we know a little more about this book, that it contains encoded messages relating to both the religious and the political histories of Western culture, but this is not the place to discuss these elements of the book in any detail. The objective here is to consider the holistic philosophy that is similarly presented within the pages of this unusual title, and determine its connection to the lost wisdom of the Ancient Celts and the prophecy of Blake.

The Preseli Triangle

Reading:

Fernacre, Rough Tor and The Great North Axis: 3:4:24-35 (Pages 81-82)

The Origin of the Preseli Triangle

Present-day awareness that there is, or could be, a Preseli Triangle arises from observations of the Stonehenge Station Stones, their relationship with the solstices, and a particular triangle, noted by astronomers as representing certain periodic movements of the moon.

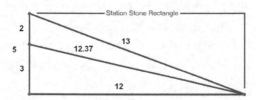

The Astronomer's Lunar Triangle

The layout above depicts this lunar triangle, which contains an outer 5:12:13 ratio Pythagorean Primitive Triad triangle. These triangles are so named because the proportions of their side lengths can always be expressed in whole numbers.

When two such triangles are rotated to fit back-to-back, so forming a rectangle, they map precisely onto the positions of the four Station Stones of Stonehenge. These stones indicate the positions of the midsummer and midwinter solstices, so relating to the Sun and the Moon in astro-geometrical terms, and these exact alignments are only applicable at the latitude upon which Stonehenge was constructed. What is particularly significant about these triangles is that, by cutting the shortest side at the 3:2 ratio point, the length of the resulting hypotenuse is 12.37, the exact number of lunar orbits in one Earth year, a period known as the synodic month.

The longer hypotenuse with the value 13 can now be considered to relate to the average lunar month of 28.02 days, (average of the synodic, sidereal and draconic), as there are 13 of these lunar months in the solar year. As these observations are also in perfect accordance with the Stonehenge calendar, it is impossible to doubt that they are inherent parts of the design of Stonehenge.

However, until recently there has been no indication that the Ancient Britons were aware of the second, shorter hypotenuse, as the 3:2 ratio point of the Station Stone rectangle does not appear to have been marked by its designers. In consequence, the general consensus amongst interested researchers and sceptics alike has been that the Station Stone Rectangle side-length ratios are merely coincidental. However, in 1997 author Robin Heath reported the discovery of a huge version of this lunar triangle in the natural landscape itself, marked out by the sacred sites of Stonehenge, Lundy Island, Caldey Island and Carn Meini, and he named the configuration *The Giant Lunation Triangle*.

Many less than critical parties have viewed Heath's claim as a testimony to a grand design of the Neolithic Celts, but, when checked with the aid of modern GPS mapping techniques, Heath's calculations have been found to be in error, with the proposed sites falling too wide of their supposed marks to be considered conclusive.

While we might be able to forgive the Ancient Celts for significant errors with regard to such massively separated landmarks, the evidence of other long-distance alignments demonstrates that these people generally attained a much higher degree of accuracy with the plotting of both straight lines and right angles than can be found in Heath's triangle. For example, even allowing for the fact that, according to Heath, whole islands have been used as landmarks, rather than specific sites such as stone circles, the distance between Carn Meini and Lundy requires Stonehenge to be sited at least eight miles further east, if the lunar triangle proportions are to be maintained. Similarly, using the distance between Carn Meini and Caldey to plot the position of Stonehenge gives an even greater error of thirteen miles.

Conversely, using the distance between Stonehenge and Lundy to plot the other two locations has the 3:2 ratio point falling in the sea well to the south of Caldey Island, a point that has never been on dry land, and finds Carn Meini over a mile to the east of its theoretical position and three miles too far north. The Celts were certainly capable of a far greater accuracy than this. And we should note that the very fact that Heath's triangle of largely natural features is not a true 5:12:13 triangle shows that, if the Celts did create a lunar triangle somewhere, it was not fortuitously based on a natural pattern of islands or other landmarks but on their knowledge of astronomy.

So, is there any truth behind the claims of an enormous lunar triangle being present in the landscape, or is this simply a starry-eyed dream of a non-existent Neolithic vision? It is just conceivable that while the "Giant Lunation Triangle" must now be viewed as disproved, the underlying principle behind Heath's idea might actually be perfectly correct. In other words, the Celts might have created a great lunation triangle of their own from scratch, and have done so on the basis of their astronomical knowledge.

It has long been a belief of this author that the alignments associated with the Preseli Cradle extend down into Cornwall, which makes the possibility of an inverted sister triangle being present in the wider landscape a prospect worthy of investigation. In recent times, the mystic Mark Lepus has discovered another, very similar triangle, through the process of 'Bluestone Channelling'. This triangle is of particular interest because it conforms to the approximate shape of the two Pythagorean Triangles that make the Station Stone rectangle, but rearranged to make one larger isosceles triangle, with an added focus that divides its centre line somewhere about the 4:8 ratio point. This point has now been dubbed the 'Divine Point' by this author. Any giant triangle of such proportions, with its most northerly point situated in the Preseli Hills, would require a North South line that extended downwards into Cornwall. The question that must now be asked is this; might it be an isosceles triangle of this specific kind that we should actually be looking for in the landscape, and if so, what is the likelihood of finding such a triangle also reflected in a specific sacred site of Western Britain?

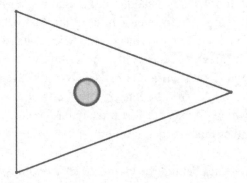

The Channelled Preseli Triangle of Mark Lepus

The starting point for such an investigation has to be the lateral line that runs east-west, between Stonehenge and Lundy Island, which should, theoretically, incorporate two more sites, the 'Divine Point' and the extreme tip of the triangle a little to the east of Stonehenge. While the latitude that Stonehenge was built on is of particular importance, the tolerance for its positioning is not all that critical. It has been demonstrated that the monument would still have functioned perfectly as a solar-lunar observatory, even if its latitude had fallen several miles further north or south. This implies that, either the Celts were aware of the concept of earth latitude, or the long-noted lateral alignment between Stonehenge and Lundy Island was purely coincidental.

The theory of the author regarding the choice of location for Stonehenge is actually a little more complex. It is always prudent to try to place oneself in the position of the people who were charged with any particularly difficult task, in order to envisage the potential practical considerations that they might have needed to incorporate into their design plan. Without doubt, they would have taken advantage of any natural features that were favourable to the development of the project. Stonehenge is situated near to the river Avon, and this would certainly have been helpful in choosing a route for bringing the stones to the site.

Further to this idea, the initial purpose of the circle and ditch construction of the outer perimeter of Stonehenge may have been to channel the flow of rainwater from the site to the river. The author can recall that, as recently as the 1960s, the winters of Britain were much colder and considerably more predictable than they are today. As a consequence, certain mischievous and forward thinking youngsters would periodically block the drain of a suitably positioned down pipe of the author's school, in order to create the perfect conditions for an ice slide to develop across the playground.

It now becomes immediately apparent that Stonehenge, and the avenue that connects it to the river, was possibly set up to take advantage of the natural lie of the land, which, with a little modification, was predisposed to the construction of a giant ice slipway. Two teams of oxen tethered to sledges, one either side of an ice road, would have had far less difficulty hauling the great stones up from the river than by use of any other means. In consequence, the final choice of position for Stonehenge would obviously have required the practical considerations of transport of so many large stones to be taken into account, whatever the method of transport, and some other, lesser marker than the monument itself may have been used to symbolize the significant outer point of the triangle.

Amazingly, the author has identified this triangle, laid out with great precision in the landscape of Western Britain, its outline being marked by three surviving hill forts. This newly discovered triangle is actually more than twice the size of the Heath triangle, stretching from Foel Drygarn in the Preseli Hills to Castle Dore on the southern coast of Cornwall, and crossing laterally from Lundy in the Bristol Channel, through the Exmoor complex, which represents the Divine Point, to terminate on the plains of Wiltshire at Quarley Hill.

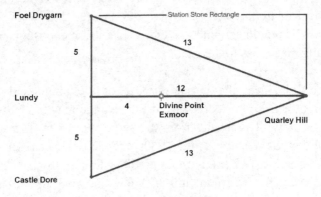

The Great Preseli Triangle

We might ask; how could the Ancient Celts possibly have positioned their monuments so accurately, without the aid of modern navigational instruments, when they were situated so far beyond the line of sight. In 3:4:33 (Page 82) *The Tome of Seus* offers us a simple answer to this puzzling question.

"By studying the sky from the ground, they learned to see the ground from the sky."

Plotting The Great Preseli Triangle

Exploring the line between Foel Drygarn and Castle Dore with the aid of modern mathematics and GPS positioning reveals that it passes right through Skull Cave on Caldey Island, a natural refuge first inhabited by the Celts some ten thousand years ago. It also passes through the promontory known as Monkstone Point, raising the possibility that this place was actually marked by a standing stone, perhaps erected by the Celtic Monks of Caldey in the early days of Christianity. The northern 3:2 ratio point actually falls in the sea, a little way North of Skull Cave, but this place would have been dry land when Caldey was first inhabited by the Ancient Celts. Several standing stones, sited on convenient high points en-route between Foel Drygarn and Monkstone Point, mark the line. It would seem that these stones, and others now presumably lost, once served as way-markers for travellers or pilgrims journeying northwards to the Preseli Cradle.

Calculating the halfway point of the line finds the precise position of Lundy Lighthouse. This represents the more southerly of the two highest natural points on Lundy of 142 metres, this one having once fallen within a 6th Century Celtic graveyard, a point that has in all certainty been an important site since the Neolithic period. The famous Lundy Inscribed Stones, currently to be found leaning against a surviving portion of the wall of the churchyard, were no doubt originally standing stones sited at the nearby high point. As was often the case in Wales and Cornwall, such standing stones were subsequently adapted for Christianity, particularly in the 6th Century, and in this case eventually relocated to their currently uncelebrated position, presumably when the lighthouse was built.

This same line also passes through the other high point on Lundy, Ackland's Moor, and is marked by a standing stone a little to the north of the lighthouse. An east-west line similarly plotted between this point and Quarley Hill passes precisely through the centre of Stonehenge, and the line between Lundy Lighthouse and Quarley passes directly through the southern entrance of Stonehenge. Such alignments might be considered coincidental, but the astonishing accuracy of these and many other associated points suggests otherwise to this author. The surprise that was experienced when these coordinates were first calculated and typed in to *Google Earth* would be hard to describe.

Continuing south, the line passes through Saint Mathiana's Well in Cornwall, which marks the 3:2 ratio point of the southern triangle, before arriving at the fort of Castle Dore some twenty three miles further on.

This north south line deviates in an anticlockwise direction from our present north south line by about 0.2 degrees, and this may either represent a minor error in the calculations of the Ancient Celts, or, alternatively, may reflect the astronomical deviation between the present time and the time of the expansion of the Preseli society. It is pertinent to mention here that the north-south orientation of Stonehenge was adjusted four times during its working life, to accommodate periodic changes in astronomical deviation.

The one thing that doesn't quite fit in this double 5:12:13 astro-geometric representation is that the position of Quarley Hill falls west of the calculated ideal position in the triangle by around 1000 yards. In view of the distances involved, about 140 miles or so in this case, and noting the fact that Quarley falls so precisely on the East West Line, the noted discrepancy with the calculated theoretical location might be considered negligible. However, it is also possible that Quarley Hill longitude was indeed determined as accurately as its latitude, and that another ancient marker, now lost to modern agriculture, once existed at this 'Mystery Point' a little to the east. Alternatively, there might be more to the story than has thus far been revealed.

A Second Interpretation of the Double Lunar Triangle

A second triangle, almost indistinguishable from the first, can be constructed by substituting the northern point of Foel Drygarn for the nearby site of Carn Meini. In contrast to the above calculations, the lines from Carn Meini to Lundy Lighthouse, and from the lighthouse to Quarley Hill, are in the precise 5:12 proportions that the lunar triangle demands. So it is conceivable that there was no error at all in the choice of location for Quarley Hill, and that its position reflects a second interpretation of the same triangle.

The 3:2 ratio point of this alternative upper lunar triangle falls in the shallow water of the main sheltered harbour of the island of Caldey, at a point that would have been dry land when the island was first settled by man, about ten thousand years ago. At the time that Stonehenge was built, this point would certainly have marked the most suitable landing point for visitors from the mainland, and would quite probably have been the site of a small harbour village, now reclaimed by the sea.

If a similar substitution is made on the southern side of this second Double Lunar Triangle, by interchanging Castle Dore for the nearby site of the well and church of the Celtic Saint Samson, the side ratios are again perfectly preserved. This time the location of the 3:2 ratio point falls in a place that has been unaffected by the rising tides of the past, and, remarkably, the line of latitude of St. Mathiana's Well cuts this line at precisely the respective calculated position.

It could again be argued that these observed correlations are purely coincidental, particularly as the angles created at Lundy by the crossing lines of this configuration make slightly less than perfect right angles in this case. This in turn creates hypotenuses in the northern and southern lunar triangles that do not quite fit the required ratio of the accepted 5:12:13 format. Until now we have been considering the geometry as measured on a flat map. However, when distances of such magnitude these are being considered, the curvature of the earth has a small but significant impact on the calculations that needs to be taken into account if absolute positions are required. In consequence, it is perfectly feasible that this second, vaguely distorted version of the Great Preseli Triangle was conceived to factor in an allowance for the curvature of the earth, where the lines of longitude move gradually closer together as they near the poles, rather than remaining parallel as on a flat map. With the northern hypotenuse appearing to be slightly stretched and the southern hypotenuse slightly compressed, when expressed on a flat map of the kind being used here, it seems that the Ancient Celts may have possessed a far greater understanding of astro-geometric science than we currently credit them with. They had, after all, used their observation of the sky in order to observe and mark out the land, a process that automatically avoids the inaccuracy inherent in the projection of maps onto flat paper.

The angle of rotation of the north-south line of this alternative representation of the Great Preseli Triangle was plotted by the author with the aid of domestic drawing instruments to be about -1.3 degrees. The calculated difference in latitudes between Carn Meini and St Samson, the most northerly and southerly points in the triangle in question is 1.6 degrees. This means that these slightly shifted flat map points do actually fit very well when real curved earth distances are being considered. Is this yet another coincidence, or were the Celtic astronomers familiar with the concepts of both flat and curved earth maps?

A Final Interpretation of the Geometry

Although the north-south lines considered so far fall extremely close to each other, they do appear to mark two distinctly separate geometric interpretations of the same essential triangle. These lines can now be thought of as being the 'Primary Line', from Foel Drygarn to Castle Dore, and the slightly rotated 'Curved Earth Line', from Carn Meini to St Samson's Well. However, there is yet another line that can be thought of as representing the north-south line of the

28

Great Preseli Triangle; the straight line that runs 2 degrees west of north to connect the tomb cairn on Carn Meini with the church of St. Veep in Cornwall. This line is also of great interest in this case, if only because it passes through such an abundance of places of significance to the Ancient Celts, and as a consequence, it has been dubbed the 'Pilgrim Line' by this author. It is interesting to note that the coordinates for the position of its southern tip, calculated from the other main points of the line, mark a place that actually lies some 150 yards or so behind the church of St Veep, to the east. While such discrepancies can be considered negligible in relation to the huge triangle that is being considered here, the possibility that there was once a holy well behind this church, at this very point, should not be ruled out.

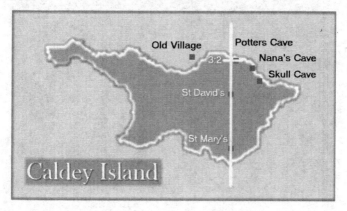

Landmarks of Caldey Island

One of the most noteworthy northerly points associated with this line is Potter's Cave on Caldey, which was first utilised by the Celtic settlers of ten thousand years ago and was certain to have been honoured by their ancestors. Although this cave does not quite fall on the line in question, it is of significance because its line of latitude cuts the Pilgrim Line precisely at the northern 3:2 ratio point.

Another important northerly location falling directly on this line is St David's Church, which the Caldey Monks tell was previously known

29

as St. Mary's by the Sea Shore, this being a small chapel dedicated to the mother of Jesus. According to the legend that they recall, this refers to a time when the present day village was a tidal inlet from the sea. However, the author is tempted to suggest that some confusion must lie behind the monk's interpretation of the legend, as neither St David's Church, nor the present day village has ever been close enough to the sea to be described in this way. Indeed, by stark contrast, in the past these places have actually been further away from the sea than they are today.

Caldey Saint David's Church

It is far more likely that the legend refers to the chapel of the old harbour village, already surmised as having existed in earlier times when the sea levels were lower. If this revised interpretation of the legend is correct, then the now lost St Mary's by the Sea, and the village of the legend, would most probably have originally marked the 3:2 ratio point of our second Great Preseli Triangle. Logically, then, the present village and chapel would have been built in the time of St David, himself a frequent visitor to the island, to replace the village and church that had been claimed by the sea.

30

This reasoning in turn implies that Christianity must have flourished in these Celtic lands long before the glorious age of the 6th century, consistently cited by historians as the period in which the early Celtic churches and associated stone relics first began to appear. In reality, the establishment of Christianity was doubtless a gradual process, and one that actually spanned the five centuries that followed its legendary introduction by Joseph of Arimathea. In all probability, the 6th Century simply marked the introduction of written ecclesiastical records, rather than the sudden and otherwise unexplained appearance of a rich, influential and highly developed theological establishment, as if from nowhere. Time and again we seem to be presented with apparent coincidences of early Christian buildings being built on former Ancient Celtic sites, and St David's Chapel, which also happens to fall on this final alignment line, is no exception.

Caldey Lighthouse now sits on the Pilgrim Line

Yet another ancient Church on Caldey was dedicated to the mother of Jesus. The Chapel of St Mary, once located on the highest point of the Island, was placed on church records by one William, Bishop of Worcester in 1490, and later mentioned by Lewis Morris in his *Plans of Harbours* of 1748. Along with St David's Church, this site also falls on the line under consideration here, the choice of high point

31

and their alignment further substantiating the likelihood of a pre Christian, Celtic connection yet again. Sadly all remains of this church were lost when the Lighthouse was built on the same spot in recent times, although the little headland below still recalls the building in its name, Chapel Point.

Using mathematics to locate the precise centre point of this final north-south line brings us next to Marisco's Castle on Lundy, raising the possibility that the castle may also have been built on an important former Celtic site. The castle was actually built by Henry III in the 13th Century, but it makes perfect sense that such an ideal location for observation, and one that is so conveniently situated to the natural safe harbour of the island, would have been utilised by the Celts from the very moment that the island was inhabited.

Travelling onwards across the Bristol Channel, the line crosses the latitude line of St Mathianna's Well at its lower 3:2 ratio point, before making its next contact at a complex of tumuli situated a little to the north of Davidstow in Cornwall. It then passes through the ancient sites of Rough Tor, Fernacre Circle and the chapel at Temple, before finally arriving at the Church of St. Veep.

The Great North Axis

Collectively, the Primary Line, the Curved Earth Line and The Pilgrim's Line mark a narrow but prominent processional path from the Preseli Cradle in the north, through to the ancient Celtic trading ports of Cornwall in the south, and in combination create the potent earth energy line first referred to in modern times, in *The Tome of Seus*, as "The Great North Axis". This is the line that many a dowser has recorded on their visits to western Britain, particularly to Lundy Island where the lines are so concentrated that even beginners can not fail to detect them. Only now is the nature of the phenomenon that these sensitive people have so often described finally becoming recognised as a most powerful, ancient and influential line of earth energy, which some say radiates for several miles in all directions.

32

What is extremely interesting to note here is that the line does not end in Cornwall. Rather, it extends downwards, touching the tip of the Breton landscape on its way to join the ancient north-south trading route that passes the length of Western Spain, to finally cross the Gibraltar Straights and meet the north coast trading route of Africa, with its long established connections through to Egypt and the Middle East. Perhaps the extended Great North Axis marks the short side of the greatest triangle of them all, completed by the line that runs between Foel Drygarn in the Preseli Hills and the Pyramids of Egypt in the East.

Geometric Conclusions

Recent research conducted by this author, and published in the title *Stonehenge Bluestone II*, has revealed that the 3:2 ratio point angle of the Lunar Triangle was actually celebrated at Stonehenge by a large Bluestone outliner, not previously associated with the monument, implying that the builders of Stonehenge were aware of the advanced astro-geometric connotations of the solar-lunar triangle. While some may consider this evidence speculative, further evidence to support the case does exist. In 2002 the author also positively identified an instance of the lunar triangle present within the stone circle of Gors Fawr in the Preseli Hills, and this circle was built about 1000 years before work on Stonehenge began. This provides conclusive proof that the Ancient Celtic people understood the complex astro-mathematical formulae that are allied to this particular triangle, long before Pythagoras rediscovered the simple geometric functions of the basic right angle triangle.

Can the same be said for the Great Preseli Triangle? Sceptics suggest that such alignments are inevitable in areas that are heavily monumented, although the accuracy of the positioning of the sites and the huge distances involved in this particular case makes that argument difficult to accept. Nonetheless, if this newly discovered Preseli Triangle could also be demonstrated to exist within the layout of one of the associated monuments, the likelihood of its attribution to coincidence would be much reduced. The first and most obvious place to look for such corroborative evidence would be the most esteemed monument of Stonehenge, and in order to facilitate this process an accurate plan of the completed monument has been reproduced below.

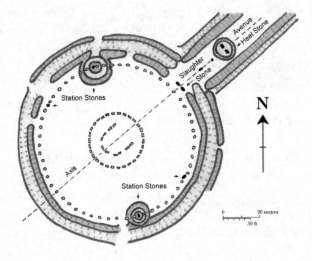

Plan of the major stones and Aubrey Holes at Stonehenge

It has long been noted that the axis of Stonehenge was set to coincide with the angle of the midsummer and midwinter solstices, and reconstructions like the one above invariably have the axis overlaid in accordance with the alignment of today. By failing to take into account the fact of an astronomical deviation, a drift of alignment taking place over many centuries, this mapping error creates the impression that the original positioning of the stones was not quite perfect. However, if we redraw the angle of axis in accordance with the original arrangement of the stones, we find that the stones were indeed perfectly aligned, but to a slightly different angle. We must therefore surmise from this observation that the angle of midsummer sunrise was, at the time of completion of the monument, very slightly different to the angle of today. Further to this observation, it must be noted that this angle of deviation plots to the very same 0.2 degrees of anticlockwise rotation that was noted in the primary example of

34

the Great Preseli Triangle, which provides further evidence of the astronomical deviation between the time of the building of Stonehenge and the present day.

The entrance to the complex falls on this axis and was marked by two stones, at the end of the avenue to the north east of the circle, one of which is known today as the Heel Stone and another which is now lost. The entrance to the outer circle was similarly marked by two more stones, one of which is lost and another, the Slaughter Stone, which is now fallen. Four additional stones, known as the Station Stones, were strategically positioned around the outer circle. These stones, together with the main central circle, represent the most fundamental elements of the monument. The obvious, elementary, conclusion to be drawn from the resultant layout is that it marked points along a processionary route that were of great importance to its users. Whether these stones held some form of theological, astronomical or perhaps sacred philosophical significance is, at this point, hard to say, but their large size doubtless provides a reflection of their importance.

Transferring these specific positions to a new layout allows the more important points to be considered in isolation. Amazingly, there, within the resultant pattern, a perfect representation of the Preseli Triangle has been present all along, quietly awaiting rediscovery since the time of the Druids.

The entrance to the complex can now be seen to mark one point of a perfectly proportioned Preseli Triangle, with two stones of the Station Stone Rectangle doubling to complete the outer frame. Furthermore, the entrance to the main Sarsen Circle, Point B, falls precisely on the 4:8 ratio point, or the Divine Point as it is now referred to here. The likelihood of the layout of these, the most important stones of the monument, being a coincidental reflection of the Preseli Triangle must now be considered infinitesimally small, particularly when the incredible accuracy of positioning is taken into account. What also becomes apparent from this layout is that the

Heel Stone and its now lost partner were positioned with similar precision, centrally between the two entrances, at Point A on the diagram below.

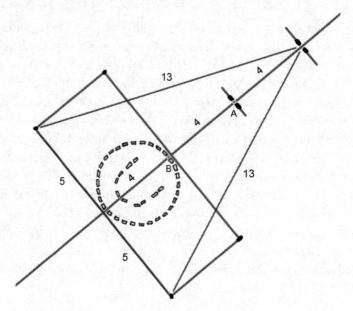

The layout of the primary stones of Stonehenge

This confirms that there were actually two 'Divine Points' in this layout, rather than just the one that had so far been determined. It may also be no coincidence that lines drawn from the centre of the circle, through the southern and western entrances, happen to pass through the two 3:2 ratio points of the Preseli Triangle.

As a consequence, it can now be stated with all confidence by this author that the Ancient Celtic People of the Preseli area must have held this particular triangle extremely sacred, so much so that they chose to incorporate a highly accurate example of it in their new temple at Stonehenge, and another magnificent, triple representation of it in the wider landscape of their homelands.

36

Holistic Reflections in the Preseli Triangle

When the 3:2 ratio points are added to the layout of the Great Preseli Triangle, it specifically integrates two smaller 3:4:5 ratio Pythagorean Primitive Triad triangles, which denote the locations of other important ancient locations. That the early Celts were aware of the mathematical properties of the Pythagorean triangle around 6000 years ago is all the more interesting since this, the simplest Pythagorean Primitive Triad triangle, became known to the people of the region now known as Iran and Iraq only about 1000 years later.

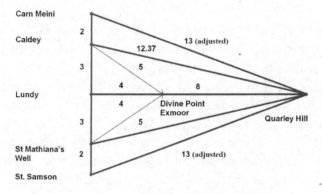

The complete Great Preseli Triangle

This lends credibility to a growing body of evidence indicating that significant cultural and trading connections were established between the Celtic Nations and the Babylonians during that period, and that these connections continued to flourish for a further three thousand years. What is particularly significant here is that it must have been the West who informed the East, rather than the other way around, as is commonly, and now clearly incorrectly, stated in many academic circles. The people of the Middle East probably used their newfound knowledge of geometry to make right-angled triangles to assist them in their construction work, just as many builders still do today, as there is currently no evidence that they used them for plotting celestial movements.

Perhaps more significantly to this case, these two smaller triangles also equate arithmetically to the Christ number, 888.

$$5 + 3 = 8$$
$$4 + 4 = 8$$
$$5 + 3 = 8$$

888 is the number of Christ according to Ancient Greek numerology. 08. 08. 08 is the publication date of *The Tome of Seus*, and the date now associated with the re-emergence of Preseli Consciousness in the modern era.

The number eight, particularly in threes, is also associated with Celtic Christianity, The Celtic Cross, the Bronze age circle of Duloe, the format of the I Ching, the concept of infinity and the now lost crosses of the Knights Templar at Temple Parish Church, Cornwall, which also falls on the Pilgrim Line of 'The Great North Axis'. The number 8, frequently expressed within a circular pattern, is also marked by innumerable Christian symbols, not least of all in the eight stained glass windows of the Methodist Chapel at Glastonbury and several of the engraved plaster wall panels of St. Illtyd's church on Caldey Island.

From the perspective of Preseli Consciousness, the Preseli Triangle clearly goes beyond the symbolism of astronomical observations. From a holistic perspective, this is the symbol of the perception and acceptance of oneness as an intellectual objective, the light that glimmers on the horizon of the path to becoming one with the universe, or one with God.

The Sun is representative of the divine male, while the Moon represents the divine female. As the Preseli Triangle embodies the entire solar-lunar dance, it is therefore symbolic of fertility and renewal, not only of mortal life, but also, more importantly, of the universe itself.

When we observe that the dance is never done, that the moon will shape the tides of the ocean tomorrow and the sun will rise once more, we are not witnessing the dance of infinity, but a truth that is held captive within the fertile age of the universe, a subject that we will return to many times in the coming pages. In consequence, the union of the Sun and the Moon, as symbolised within the Preseli Triangle, ultimately represents the transcendence of all the yin-yang characteristics of mortal being, (Male and Female, Rational and Intuitive, Good and Evil) and the acceptance of an Intelligence that surpasses the necessities that determine mortal life in this universe.

The Great North Axis
(Coordinates in Google Earth format)

Primary Line (-0.2 degrees North South Line)
Foel Drygarn 51.970222,-4.683373
Monkstone Point 51.696984,-4.679690
Caldey Skull Cave 51.639387,-4.679691
Lundy Ackland's Moor 51.172132,-4.674082
Lundy Lighthouse 51.167171,-4.673658
Saint Mathiana's Well 50.684314,-4.675421 southern 3:2 point
Castle Dore 50.362738,-4.667902

Curved Earth Line (-1.3 degrees North South Line)

Carn Meini 51.961101,-4.704892
Caldey Old Harbour Northern 3:2 point (calculated) 51.64215,-4.692707
Lundy Lighthouse 51.167171,-4.673658
Saint Mathiana's Well 50.684314,-4.675421 (cuts at the southern 3:2 point)
St Samson's Well: 50.366348,-4.643966

The Pilgrim Line (-2 degrees North South Line)

Bedd Esus 51.960852,-4.708044
Potter's Cave 51.641710,-4.684309 (cuts the line at the northern 3:2 point)
Caldey St. David's Church 51.637837,-4.685154
Caldey Lighthouse 51.631636,-4.684765
Lundy Marisco's Castle 51.163235,-4.6608155
Davidstow Tumuli Complex 50.664968,-4.623013
Rough Tor 50.597077,-4.622488
Fernacre Circle 50.589984,-4.622441
Saint Mathiana's Well 50.684314,-4.675421 (cuts at the southern 3:2 point)
Temple Chapel 50.529491,-4.617015 southern 4:1 ratio point
St. Veep Church 50.365373,-4.616739 or
Possible lost well (calculated) 50.365618,-4.613587

Other Sites of Interest

Carn Meini Menhir: 51.960553,-4.704962
Carnalw 51.970532,-4.710625
Stone River Large Stone 51.959769,-4.710096
Carn Bica 51.959682,-4.724073
Bedd Arthur 51.959553,-4.7223
Waun Lwyd Doorway Markers 51.94924,-4.681984
Caldey Nanna's Cave 51.640884,-4.68108
Avebury: 51.428648,-1.854029

The Pilgrimage

Reading:

Carn Meini from Efailwen: 3:7:17 (Page 90)
The First Stonehenge: 1:4:30 (Page 15)
The enlightenment of Esus: 1:4:26-28 (Page 15)
Stone River Explained: 1:9:26-27 (Page 34) and 6:7:9 (Page173)

The Great North Axis

The Great North Axis has been identified as marking the most important trade route of the Celtic people of ancient times, stretching from Scotland in the north through to Bretton and Galacia in the south, and creating a significant section of one of the two routes for the tin of Cornwall and Spain to the Middle East. It also served as an important element of the trade routes from the south into Ireland and formed the most northerly section of the Phoenician trade routes from the Mediterranean. Records show that these Celtic links actually remained unbroken until modern times, extending into the twentieth century when the arrival of the railways finally spelled ruin for the inland port of Haverfordwest.

It follows, therefore, that this route, with its established conveniences for travellers, would have also served the needs of spiritual travellers and provided the most eminent thinkers of the day with a logistical

41

artery for the dissemination of their grand vision. In order to develop the picture further, it now becomes vital to take a closer look at some of the individual sites of this long-lived information highway, particularly as there is evidence to show that its period of theological importance extended well into the Christian era.

The Sites of Cornwall

The most southerly points of the Great Preseli Triangle are Castle Dore, which is situated on the western side of the Fowey estuary in Cornwall, and St Veep Church, which lies on the eastern bank. The church began as a hermitage in the sixth century and, although it survives to this day, very little is known about the particular Celtic Christian Saint who was responsible for its establishment. It is said that he, or she, was a member of the family of the Welsh King Brychan of Brycheiniog, modern day Breconshire.

Saint Veep was almost certainly an associate of Saint Samson, who, along with Saint David, had a mission to take the word of their belief system from the sacred lands of South West Wales to the wider world. While Saint David went east to found Glastonbury Church and then meet the Christians of Rome, Saint Samson followed the Great North Axis southward, eventually to become Bishop of Dol, in Brittany, setting up churches in Cornwall and Guernsey along the way. Given his association with Caldey Island, it is probably no coincidence that Saint Samson's first settling point on his journey was the southern tip of the Great Preseli Triangle, precisely between the locations of the church of Saint Veep and Quarley Hill. He is still remembered there in the name of the church that he founded in the village of Golant, and in the ancient holy well, St Samson's Well.

The old wells of Britain would have been frequently visited by the local inhabitants and would therefore have provided ideal places for the early saints to establish their primitive hermitages. Some historians suggest that the Celtic Saints chose to set up their practices by these wells for purely practical reasons, but the sites were almost certainly chosen as much because they were already long-recognised holy places as for their practical use in supplying the local community with drinking water. Supporting this assessment is the fact that in Christian, and other, symbology water, that essential for human life, and especially flowing water, has long been taken as representing the holy spirit.

Bronze Statue of Saint Samson on Caldey Island

Moving northwards along the Pilgrim Line, towards the Preseli Cradle from Saint Veep, the next place of significance is St Catherine's Church in the remote Cornish hamlet of Temple. This little chapel is actually built on an earlier site, the original sanctuary having been commissioned by the Knights Templar during the 12th Century, in what was then an isolated location on the moors. Why they chose this specific lonely and windswept place to build a temple is not recorded, although the popular explanation purports that it was to provide pilgrims with a refuge on their journey between Ireland and the Holy Land.

In truth, this practice appears to have begun after ownership of the temple passed into the hands of the 'Knights Hospitallers' when the Knights Templar were disbanded in 1312. However, the alignment of the location not only falls along the The Great North Axis but also cuts the southern portion of the 'Pilgrim Line' (Carn Meini to St. Veep) at precisely the 4:1 ratio point, which is unlikely to be mere coincidence. When this observation is coupled with that of Dr John Langdon Down, who recorded before his demise in 1896 that the churchyard had originally contained eight stone crosses, it suggests that the Templars' interest in the site may have been associated with their Ancient Celtic heritage and its Christ connection.

Moving further north across the moors the line in question passes through the centre of Fernacre Circle. This location was, without doubt, chosen for this monument specifically because it falls in centrally with three natural markers of the cardinal points of the compass; Rough Tor to the north, also on the ley line, Brown Willy to the east and Garrow Tor to the south. Although the western cardinal was not marked by any natural rock formation, the choice of location for Stannon Circle provided the fourth, man-made mark in precisely this direction.

To the west we also find the large settlement at Louden Hill, which falls in the approximate direction of a settlement alleged in *The Tome of Seus* to include the Cornish mansion of the father of Jesus. If this claim is correct, and *The Tome of Seus* has been proved correct in many similarly surprising instances, Louden Hill or some other very nearby site, would have been the seat of King Cynfelyn in Cornwall, and the seat of Arviragus, King of Cornwall after that, long before the Arthurian legends ever came into being. This place may then be the original Camalot, of which Tintagel would have become an important outlying part, along with St Michael's Mount where the ingots of tin were held in safekeeping in preparation for their shipment to Turkey. Much evidence to support this case is revealed and discussed in *The Final Conclusion* of the last chapter of the book *The Almighty King*.

To the north, the summit cairn of Rough Tor stands precisely on the Preseli to St Veep line and is surrounded by walls and cairns, many now collapsed, which once combined with the natural granite rock features of the site to create a labyrinth of enclosures. On a clear day the view from this site is outstanding, and between 3500 and 4000 BC, when the complex was first completed, it would surely have been a very important place. Whilst occupation at Rough Tor has been dated to the Neolithic period there are indications that it may have been in use during the Bronze Age and again later, in the Mediaeval period, when a chapel dedicated to St Michael was built near the summit.

Further north, the latitude line of the holy well known as St Mathianna's cuts the southern portion of this line at precisely the 3:2 ratio point. According to both Cornish and Breton traditions, Anna was the grandmother of Jesus, who fled Cornwall for Judea when her royal husband became extremely displeased with her. She eventually returned to Cornwall and set up residence on the island of Lamanna, modern-day St George's Island, where she was visited by Jesus. Many churches and place names in Cornwall are dedicated to Saint Anna, and, as Mathianna means 'Mother Anna', this holy well is probably no exception. What is of particular interest about this story is that it provides a possible major Christ connection at a highly significant sacred geometric position.

Lundy Island

The next location appearing along this northward journey is the Island of Lundy in the Bristol Channel. Lundy has been used as a steppingstone between Cornwall and Wales by Celtic mariners for thousands of years and its mysterious otherworldly atmosphere has attracted the attention of spiritual pilgrims to this day. A recent study of the island's standing stones by Robert W. E. Farrah, who once kept the lighthouse there, has revealed that the ancient inhabitants of Lundy had arranged the stones to function as a solar calendar. Alignments with the mainland in Devon were also discovered, and two further north-south alignments, which clearly denote the Great North Axis. It is interesting to note that, on a particularly clear day, Exmoor to the East, the Preseli Hills to the north and Cornwall to the south are all visible from Ackland's Moor on Lundy.

Robert Farrah has also written a second paper on Lundy, *Symbolic Alignment of St Helena's Church*, which provides evidence for the continuous application of esoteric knowledge in the alignments of sacred monuments throughout the whole period of the Celtic Ancestors and that of the Celtic Christians who succeeded them.

Caldey Island

Before arriving at mainland Wales, The Great North Axis crosses the sacred island of Caldey. *The Life of Paul Aurelian*, completed in 884 by a monk named Wrmonoc from Breton, tells the story of one of seven Welsh saints who took Celtic Christianity to North West France in the sixth century. From this work we learn that Caldey was once named Ynnys Pyr and that St Illtyd, St David, St Paul, St Gildas, and St Samson, amongst others, frequently convened at the monastery there in the years which preceded the Celtic Christian mission to Brittany. It would seem therefore that Caldey Island had been in the possession of the Celtic Church for some time prior to this period, and that it represented the primary meeting place for the most learned Celtic Christians of the era.

The various lives of St Samson, essentially derived from the memoir of a relative by the name of Enoch, who was in turn informed by the saint's mother Anne, tell us that a monk named Pyro had established a monastery there in an earlier time. According to Enoch, Abbot Pyro was partial to a tipple, and one dark night he fell into the monastery well in a drunken stupor. The other monks heard his cry for help but, despite being successfully rescued, he died of his injuries some hours later. Pyro was almost certainly remembered in the name of the island, Ynys Pyr, as much as for the unfortunate circumstances of his untimely demise. There is no record of the name of the island prior to the arrival of Pyro, but it is likely that a small church, probably the one originally dedicated to Saint Mary that was relocated in the sixth century, predated the monastery, which implies that the island has a very long Christian history indeed.

The young St Samson was chosen to succeed Pyro and was ordained by the Archbishop Dubricius, who was also on the island at that time, and St Samson served as Abbot for three more years. Analysis of these early written records has led some religious historians to conclude that Caldey was the most significant and sacred place of the early Celtic Christians, and that St Illtyd's monastery in Llantwit, which is generally believed to have been the primary Christian centre in Britain at that time, was actually of secondary importance to Caldey. It should be remembered that this history is actually the history of later Celtic Christianity, as it was soon to be wiped out by the Roman Christian invasion of AD 597, and that the earlier history was unfortunately not documented. It is also worthy of note that this particular history also predates the establishment of the abbey at Glastonbury by Saint David, after he left South West Wales to spread the word of his faith.

The 3:2 point of the northern portion of the Pilgrim Line takes us to Potter's Cave, one of three surviving caves on Caldey Island that were inhabited from early times. Evidence unearthed at the caves of Caldey by the Cambrian Archaeological Association has revealed that its Neolithic inhabitants of around 9000 years ago were already a socially advanced people. On page six of his book, *Caldey, An Island of the Saints*, the Rev. William Done Bushell summarises the findings of their work.

There was also evidence of a 'flint factory'. From the animal bones discovered it was possible to trace the arrival of the domestic dog, affording, it is thought, the first instance in Britain of its association with man during one of the stages of the Mesolithic cultural development.

Nanna's Cave on Caldey Island

Several other nearby caves were lost when the area below Potter's cave was turned into a limestone quarry in more modern times, but Nanna's Cave, named in the 1960s by the archaeologists who found the skeleton of a woman there, remains a popular location for pilgrims and tourists alike.

Travellers of today who venture onward along the Pilgrim Line will first clasp eyes on Carn Meini as they reach the crown of the hill on the main road at Efailwen. At a little over 1200 feet above sea level, Carn Meini is certainly no towering mountain peak, but somehow the distinctive outline of this otherwise unassuming summit has the power to conjure an inexplicable sense of awe and wonder in the hearts of its pilgrims. Whatever the weather, the light that cushions this sleeping dragon of Wales is always something of a surprise to behold. Some seem able to sense its presence even before they glimpse its serene shape, waiting patiently in the milky distance, with many experiencing the onset of an overwhelming sense of anticipation and excitement from the first moment that they join the northward track.

The classic view of Carn Meini from the South

Leaving the menhirs of Efailwen Summit behind, the pilgrims of old would have had no further need of way markers. Spurred on by the iconic vision before them, their journeys would have been simply completed by one of the most direct and easiest routes before them. Some would have followed the track that is still remembered by the road of today, from Glandy Cross to Mynachlogddu. Others may have preferred to trek across the moors, passing by the ancient circle of Gors Fawr as they went. Either way, the traveller of yesteryear would have ultimately encountered the now ancient path that winds its way through the Preseli Cradle to connect the three terminal sites of the Great North Axis, the Tomb of Carn Meini, the mount itself and Foel Drygarn.

Carn Meini Tomb, dubbed 'Bedd Esus' by the author

The Tomb of Carn Meini

The tomb of Carn Meini heads the Pilgrim Line and is often the first monument on the mount to be encountered by the visitors of today. Initially, the old path makes straight for a crossing point at the 'River of Stones', a long, dense arc of precariously positioned rocks that lead directly to the burial chamber above. Though partly collapsed, the tomb remains a splendid example of a chambered cairn, and, being the only tomb on the mount, it was clearly the burial place of an extremely significant person in the history of the early Celtic settlers. The importance of the Preseli area, as a cradle of astronomy, engineering and socio-theological developments, cannot be overstated. It is probable that this is either the grave of a great king, or of the enlightened individual who first conceived the grand philosophical notion of society and its relationship with the universe that gave rise to the golden era of Neolithic advancement. This place, then, may be the grave of the forefather of the Druids.

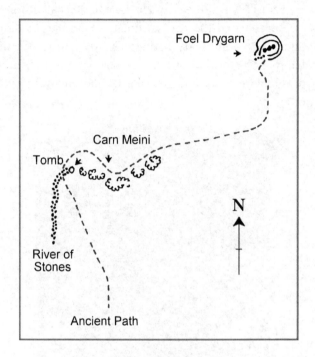

Monuments of the Preseli Cradle

According to *The Tome of Seus*, that person was called Esus, Esus being a Celtic Sage who, fortunately for the historic records, was immortalised in later times in two carved stone columns in France, the most famous of which was rediscovered in Paris in the 18th century beneath the Cathedral of Notre Dame. If Esus was indeed an early Celtic Deity of the Neolithic Golden Age, then it appears that his role was corrupted in later times. During the Celtic-Romano period he took on a more pagan God-like role, and was severely demonised by the first century Roman poet Marcus Annaeus Lucanus, or Lucan as he is better known. It is impossible to imagine that the early Celtic Christians were the willing inheritors of the sacred sites of so depraved a heritage as that claimed by the Romans.

51

While it is to be expected that a Roman poet of that era would adopt the propagandist tactic of declaring the Celts vile advocates of such evil practices as human sacrifice, Lucan's commentary is not necessarily entirely void of value. He connects Esus with the Druids and so, reading beyond the corrupt image of Roman making which portrays them as blood-thirsty barbarians, we can deduce that Esus was probably a historic Celtic character who was held in high esteem, presumably with good reason, by the educated elite of the times, the Druids.

The Esus column of Paris

Purported evidence of Celtic human sacrifice is sometimes claimed also as evidence of the worship of Esus in Britain, although, in reality, there is no evidence that Esus, or any other of the so-called

Celtic Gods, were actually worshiped at all. It is equally likely that these were real people, who were simply cherished as wise ancestors, or celebrated as great deities for reasons that are now forgotten. In *A Dictionary of Celtic Mythology* James MacKillop explains the case for Esus worship.

> Although Esus' cult was thought confined to Gaul, the discovery of Lindow Man, the body of an ancient human sacrifice found in Cheshire in 1984, implied to some commentators the propitiation of Esus in Britain.

The view that the alleged Druidic associations with cannibalism and human sacrifice were in fact initiated by the Romans to motivate their soldiers and justify murderous invasion policies is gradually gaining acceptance. This realisation is largely due to the insistence of amateur archaeologists that no real evidence exists, other than the untrustworthy tales of the brutal invaders themselves, who, despite their own incomparably depraved history, are still frequently stated to have civilised the British. However, interpretation of a relatively new find of human bones from this era in National Geographic's *Great Druid Massacre*, a documentary guided by a group of professional archaeologists, has resurrected the old argument, suggesting that the Romans may have been telling the truth about the Celts all along.

The bones in question were originally discovered in a crevasse in Alveston, Gloucestershire, by two potholers, who realised the significance of the hoard when they uncovered a human skull in the murky depths of the cave. Subsequent excavations revealed that the bones were of a large number of Celtic Britons, over one hundred in number, all of whom had met violent deaths, their dismembered remains having then been pushed through a narrow entrance into the cave system below.

To find so many human bones from this period, while unusual, is not remarkable, but this particular find stood out from others of its type in the Celtic world. One of the long bones was split longitudinally, suggesting to the excavators that this bone had been deliberately opened in such a way as to provide access to the marrow inside. This they believed could only be associated with one thing, cannibalism, an act that was, in this case, probably executed as part of a desperate Druidic ritual to implore their Gods for assistance in the face of the advancing Roman Legions.

Also found among the remains were the bones of dogs, a fact which the team coupled with a quite separate, unconnected find from another part of Britain of a beautifully cast bronze greyhound figurine, to claim that the Ancient Celts had believed in a dog God!

This author contends that a number of aspects of the interpretation do not ring true. Firstly, all the human skeletons were of adults who, apart from the fact that their wounds are, reportedly, of the classic battle type, appeared to have been basically fit and healthy prior to their deaths. Previous interpretations of similar finds have been that the bones were of the victims of a battle, rather than of barbaric rituals.

Rival communities in Ancient France were known to have engaged in battles that resulted in similarly high casualty figures, but, while the victors were known for utilising the remains of their foes as trophies, the dispassionate dismembering and disposal of the bodies in this way is unheard of. A more likely explanation for the Alveston case would be that the victims died while defending their community against the Roman advance, and that the victors subsequently dismembered their remains in order to facilitate their disposal through the narrow entrance of a convenient nearby cave system. Dating of the bones supports this view. Furthermore, some of the bodies were of women, and we know from Roman accounts of the period that the Celtic people were prepared to send their women into battle in such dire circumstances. Painstaking reconstruction of one of the skulls also showed evidence of a deathblow inflicted by a sharp and heavy implement, this being entirely in keeping with the trauma caused by a Roman sword during battle.

The reason for the bones of large dogs being present at the site could also have another, perhaps more practical, explanation. Dogs would have been kept by many communities at that time, both for hunting and for security, and would have played a far more important role in the community than ever they do today. Any group of people facing the prospect of a battle in which they were to be greatly outnumbered would have been foolish not to consider all possible strategic advantages at their disposal, and that would undoubtedly have included the deployment of their fierce and trusty dogs as co-warriors. The bodies of the dogs could simply have been collected with the others and disposed of at the same time.

The large number of people involved would represent the entire battle-capable sector of a typical Celtic settlement, and it seems unlikely that any community would favour a sacrificial ritual which called for the total annihilation of the only people capable of defending them, particularly at such a desperate time.

So far, this brief re-appraisal of the evidence suggests that the more traditional interpretation, that the bones were of battle victims, is by far the more likely, but for one critical piece of evidence, the longitudinal fracture of a human long bone.

The archaeologists in question insisted that any bone which has had the ends removed and also been split along its length must be evidence of removing the marrow for food. Did they investigate other possible explanations before arriving at a final verdict, or is this just an unsubstantiated opinion resulting in a determination to reach a predetermined preferred conclusion, thus perpetuating the myth that the Romans civilized the uneducated savages of Britain? Are the professionals assuming, as they so often do, what they want to prove?

For this author, many reservations remain. If the bone had been split for food, why would it be the only bone exhibiting signs of cannibalism? Is it plausible that someone charged with the disposal of so many bodies would have taken the time to separate a single limb and consume the flesh raw, and then suck out the marrow? If not, there must be another logical explanation.

Investigation of modern medical reports shows that ordinary, accidental longitudinal fractures of long bones are uncommon, but by no means unheard of. The bones of healthy young people have been recorded as having fractured in this way simply as a result of vigorous exercise. Forensic reports show that bones can split when damaged by sharp implements and one butcher I spoke to explained to me exactly how this might happen.

In order to render the bodies suitable for disposal in the cave they would probably have been cut into sections using a sharp heavy implement, such as a Roman sword or an axe. Dismembering at the joints would have been tedious in such circumstances and so cuts below and above the joints would be expected. When such a cut is made, with a heavy cleaver in the case of a butcher, the implement may not always cut through the limb in one go, sometimes coming to rest half way through the bone. At this point there is a temptation to rock the blade sideways before removing it. This has the effect of opening the incision, thereby facilitating a clean second cut, and can sometimes result in the longitudinal splitting of the bone.

This indicates that bones that had split longitudinally would probably be found in small numbers amongst the remains of people whose bodies have been despatched in this way, and their presence is therefore not indicative of either cannibalism or sacrificial ceremonies.

Predictably, perhaps, the documentary also uses the supposedly 'classic case' of Lindow Man to further the programme makers' argument for sacrificial Druidic rites. Until its recent discovery, the body of Lindow Man had lain preserved in a Cheshire peat bog since a time before the Roman northern advance. The man had been killed by three methods, a fact given great significance in the documentary. These 'three deaths' were considered a feature of Druidic sacrificial practice on account of the Druids' alleged attribution of magical significance to the number three, but no evidence for this claim was provided. We should perhaps ask these archaeologists whether those who were later hung, drawn and quartered during the Middle Ages were in reality despatched by mediaeval Druids? The notion that the Druids had been capable of such acts is a gross libel of peaceable people from the mouths of those who did indeed resort to similar barbarities, even millennia later.

While the Druids may have provided moral support and advice to their Chieftains during the Roman invasion, and intervened at times of intertribal friction in order to avoid bloodshed, there is no evidence to suggest that they had any jurisdiction over community law. Presumably, therefore, it was the tribal Kings who administered justice. The individual found in the peat bog could easily have been the recipient of an unwelcome punishment, rather than a willing sacrifice, as has been suggested. Retribution for crimes like betrayal, murder and theft is, even today in some parts of the world, still exacted according to the principle of an eye for an eye. There may have been rare circumstances, such as treachery, for example, where such punishments were administered by the Ancient Celts.

That the victim was found to have mistletoe berries in his stomach may, conceivably, be indicative of some form of Druidic involvement in his death, as Druids are said to have used the berries in their ceremonies, but there is no actual bona fide evidence of this. In an unconnected process, Druidic practitioners could have simply previously prescribed mistletoe berries as a medication. Alternatively, the berries might have been administered as part of a 'right of passage' for a political traitor, prior to the administration of punishment, in a process akin to the modern religious practice of sprinkling holy water on a condemned man, but this would not mean that the priest was responsible for his dispatch.

Author David Jones offers a different, but equally plausible, explanation for the death of Lindow Man in his book *Footprints in the Stone.*

It was then alleged, because the ritual killing of 150 Britons did not work, and the Romans were still marching to Anglesey, the Druids ritually killed a high status Briton (Lindow Man). It was also said that this was a 3 death ritual killing, because Lindow Man was bludgeoned, garrotted and had his throat cut; and also had 4 mistletoe pollens in his stomach.

Is the latter TV presenter's three death ritual theory of Lindow Man realistic or any other theory for that matter?

Accordingly, should the Druids have killed 3 people? Or is it a better explanation that this high status Briton was tortured by the Romans?

The evidence is, he was smashed on the head twice (is not any Celtic 3) then slowly torque garrotted, with his hands tied behind his back, possibly to gain information of the Britons whereabouts and strengths, and when nothing came forth, the Romans cut his throat for good measure and tossed him into the bog.

The presenter's mistletoe theory is also suspect, why 4 grains of pollen (why not the Celtic 5)? Is it simply possible that this pollen was used in a medicine preparation, or a fruit brew, or cooking procedure, which Lindow man had for lunch?

While supposition, conjecture and speculation are important parts of the investigation process, it is far better to label the type of thinking used in the documentary accordingly, rather than to claim to have penned a new chapter of knowledge on the Druids, which is, once again, based on ill-considered evidence and poorly grounded conclusions.

In *The Tome of Seus*, Esus was enlightened on Carn Meini when he broke open a stone on the mount and saw the 'seeds of serenity' within. He then retired to the woods to consider what he had seen, and there, living as a woodsman, he presumably learned much from the animals, from nature and from quiet contemplation of the universe. Eventually, he emerged as an enlightened soul and took his wisdom to the people. If the title of the book is to be considered a euphemism for, or pun on, the 'Tomb of Esus', then it is certain the book is suggesting that the tomb of Carn Meini is the grave of Esus. While this may or may not be precisely the historical truth, the idea that this is the tomb of an important Celtic deity has already been shown highly likely, and, as Esus is the most eminent deity to have survived on record, this contention is well within the bounds of possibility.

The book goes on to tell us that this particular Esus commissioned the building of Stonehenge, initially from four score stones of Carn Meini, and that he was eventually buried at the new monument. This clearly implies that the earliest holes at Stonehenge, the 'Aubrey Holes', were excavated as sockets for the Bluestones from the outset, and not for wooden posts, as previously thought. In consequence, if the book were to be found correct on this point, the date of the arrival of the Bluestones on the Wiltshire Downs would have to be pushed back by approximately 500 years.

In September 2008, however, in contradiction of this hypothesis, archaeologists Wainwright and Darvill announced to the world in their first BBC Stonehenge documentary that the Bluestones arrived much later than previously thought. This contention was based on the carbon dating of organic material excavated from beneath one of the Bluestones at Stonehenge, which determined its erection at about 2300 BC, a clear implicit claim that the hypothesis of *The Tome of Seus* was incorrect.

Being aware of the 'Seus Hypothesis' by this time, this author submitted a report to the BBC Stonehenge Documentary Forum, outlining an alternative theory and pointing out that Wainwright and Darvill had only managed to date the last erection of the single Bluestone in question (the Bluestones being known to have been taken down and re-erected several times) and not the date they were first erected at Stonehenge.

That message was never published on the forum, (though it was published elsewhere) nor was it ever acknowledged by the BBC, an interesting instance of censorship of a dissenting voice. However, on Monday 01 June 2009, BBC Channel 4 issued a second documentary entitled *The Secrets of Stonehenge*, in which Wainwright and Darvill abandoned their claim, made only nine months earlier, and stated that the Bluestones had actually arrived earlier than previously thought, not later. Unsurprisingly, this conclusion was reached after the further excavation and analysis of one of the Aubrey Holes, in which fragments of Bluestone were discovered. Unfortunately, neither of the archaeologists made any reference to their earlier errors of judgement, and the 'remarkable discovery' that Stonehenge was actually older than previously thought was passed off as if it had been entirely their own. It now appears that the archaeological community generally accepts this 'new' theory, and therefore implicitly acknowledges that some time before their own pronouncement *The Tome of Seus* had indeed been quite correct on the point.

As Wainwright and Darvill have effectively proved the hypothesis in *The Tome of Seus* to be accurate, it must now be considered possible that the book was also correct in its other contention, that Esus, the father of Preseli Consciousness, was actually buried there. The remains of Esus would have needed to be exhumed from their original place of rest on Carn Meini, and transported to Stonehenge, after a substantial passage of time, since Stonehenge took well over a thousand years to complete in its entirety, even its first phase being, perhaps, hundreds of years in the making.

In general terms, the raiders of remote and ancient graves like the one on Carn Meini, now dubbed 'Bedd Esus', have tended to be the archaeologists of the modern age. In consequence, the fact that no body has ever been found at the Carn Meini tomb might indicate that the monument had been built as only a temporary sanctuary, no matter how grand it might have been. It is interesting to note that this particular grave was the focus of a recent excavation by Professors Wainwright and Darvill, who have since suggested that it may be the grave of the architect of Stonehenge, once again, exactly as implied in *The Tome of Seus*. As the book came before their investigations and proclamations, one is forced to wonder whether these people used it as a source of inspiration, or even whether they are tuning in to the conversations and writings of those of us who have?

As a final note on the subject of the relics of Esus, *The Tome of Seus* quite clearly states that his remains were eventually re-buried at Stonehenge. If this was indeed the case, there is just a chance that the skeleton of a man that was previously excavated at Stonehenge, which is now held in the museum at Salisbury, is actually the remains of the father of Preseli Consciousness, who laid the footstones upon which so many philosophers, mathematicians and scientists were later to tread. Other bodies have been exhumed there, but this one was particularly well preserved and deemed to be the remains of an extremely important person. Modern forensic techniques can sometimes determine the birthplace of a person from skeletal remnants, even when buried elsewhere, by analysis of the fluoride content of the teeth, while radiocarbon dating can establish the approximate date at which they lived. If the Salisbury skeleton could be proved to have originated in the Preseli area, and to be older than the organic material buried with it, this would establish that this person was not only re-interred, but was in all probability the man referred to in *The Tome of Seus* as Esus. This skeleton may therefore be the most sacred of relics for the people of the Celtic race. The Celtic World must now hope that these bones, and other skeletal remains exhumed from Stonehenge, will eventually become the subjects of appropriate forensic tests.

Before moving up and across Carn Meini to the final location of the pilgrimage, a few words will be spent in consideration of the purpose of the highly unusual monument known as the 'River of Stones'. No official attempt appears to have been made by the archaeological community to solve this riddle, and little else in the way of hypotheses has been offered by the amateur sector. As a consequence, it occurred to the author that there might be some kind of reference to the River of Stones in *The Tome of Seus*, particularly if the title of the book was intended to draw attention to the tomb on Carn Meini. Sure enough, there appear to be two references in the book to this rocky road amidst the Preseli Hills, which collectively offer a perfectly plausible explanation for its creation.

In the first reference, 1:9:26-27, we learn that the stones refer to the fertile age of the Universe, the period during which the universe is capable of supporting life, with Earth representing just one stone or step in the long and difficult journey of evolution. We are also reminded that our ultimate survival on this immeasurably long trek is currently dependent upon our responsibility as caretakers of our planet, which in the present micro-phase of reckless consumerism paints a picture of the future that is very frightening indeed.

Reading on into the second passage, 6:7:9, we discover that the pilgrimage of each individual is a metaphor for the journey of their life, and that each stone that they lay, or life that they lead, is part of the greater journey of life on Earth.

Collectively, therefore, the stones present a metaphorical representation of the steps that we must tread, or the lives that we must lead, to reach salvation. In a more literal sense, the stones are the offerings of individuals who have committed themselves to seek the truth, through application of the philosophy of Esus, each stone having been laid by an individual in the final leg of their pilgrimage to the tomb.

The more stones that are laid the greater will be our appreciation of the enormity of the journey, from primitive life to the redemption of the eternal soul, a journey that must be completed within the timescale of the fertile age if we are ultimately to survive. Anyone who has actually attempted to walk this stony path to the tomb above will certainly gain a greater understanding of the meaning of the passage in the book.

It is fascinating to note that this is a practice that appears to have been revived in modern times, with stones having been identified by the author as originating from as far afield as the Lake District. This is presumably because pilgrims now have the advantage of travelling by motor vehicle. It is also quite ironic to consider that, in this new and troubled era, some people are bringing stones from considerable distances to leave at the site, while others are stealing stones from the mount and then smashing them to sell the pieces, for a profit, to people who live far away.

If, as the book states, the River of Stones was actually constructed by the pilgrims of old, it is rational to believe that this custom was instigated while the architect of the ritual was actually still alive, as it was a task of the Esus of *The Tome of Seus* to find a practical way to reveal the path to the people. Since the recent excavation of Bedd Esus, the tomb of Carn Meini, Professors Wainwright and Darvill have reliably informed us that there is a ceremonial Bluestone earthwork situated beneath the tomb. As it was the original head of the River of Stones it may well have been symbolic of the ultimate goal at the end of the journey, perhaps representing the attainment of spiritual unity for all life in this universe, since bluestone shows a starry heaven to which all conscious beings aspire. Equally, but less romantically, it is possible that the tomb was erected on the site of an earlier burial place, after the body had been removed to be reinterred elsewhere, to provide a fitting memorial at the site of the original burial.

While Bedd Esus may be representative of the ultimate valid goal of humanity, it does not appear to have been the final monument of the pilgrimage, at least not in the later times of the Bronze Age. The old path actually presses onward, crossing the level ground at the summit of Carn Meini finally to reach its end at the hill fort of Foel Drygarn.

Foel Drygarn

Foel Drygarn is generally considered to be a Bronze Age hill fort and the paths that lead upward to the monument are certainly sufficiently steep to leave visitors breathless upon arrival. Three impressive stone cairns crown the summit of this windy and seemingly inhospitable hill, but Foel Drygarn has a mysterious and intriguing charm that somehow seems to win over those who rise to the challenge of the climb.

With regard to the name, Foel translates as bald, from the word moel, which in this context means bare hilltop. The word Drygarn may have originally referred to the three cairns of the summit, but, as Wyn Owens, local historian from Mynachlogddu, says, "to be pedantic, three cairns would translate from 'tair carn', so, although three cairns seems to be the likely meaning, we can't actually be sure of that".

The now familiar alignment of Foel Drygarn and the two other forts of the Great Preseli Triangle, Quarley Hill and Castle Dore, indicate the reality of a continuous Preseli Consciousness throughout the Neolithic and Bronze Ages. In view of the fact that the nearby Neolithic circle of Gors Fawr incorporates a lunar triangle of comparable proportions, it should also be considered that these three Bronze Age sites might have been constructed on former, perhaps less developed but similarly important, Neolithic sites.

However, Foel Drygarn does not appear to fit well with the accepted format of the Bronze Age fort, although it has been claimed that aerial photographs reveal the remains of a number of roundhouses, and it does possess an outer and inner wall, of sorts. This claim is hard to support even so, as there is just one circle that fits the description of a roundhouse (differing colour of vegetation and accurate circular foundations) with a viable inner diameter of about 20 feet. While such a building could have been used as a dwelling, it would not be adequate to support a community of the size that would be associated with a hill fort, nor does the exposed and hostile nature of the location render it suitable for a conventional settlement of any kind.

While a number of smaller circles are identifiable, they are of a similar appearance to several that occur outside the fort, suggesting that they are either small temporary shelters from the winds for visitors to the summit, or possibly the remnants of pits that were used to provide the source material for the earthworks at the site. The second of these possibilities seems quite likely, as most of the circles are conveniently situated near the parts of the site that would have needed to be significantly raised during construction.

As the evidence of the single roundhouse is patently inadequate to support a viable hamlet community, it seems probable that it was used to house a smaller, more select group of people, who presumably either visited periodically or acted as caretakers to the site. Equally, if this was not a settlement in the usual sense, it follows that the walls were not used for defence purposes. Without adequate manpower to police them, the walls would have provided a wholly ineffective means of defence against any desperate or opportunist invaders. So, if this thinking is on the correct lines, we are left with a puzzling situation. The walls must have taken a considerable amount of time and effort to construct, so why were they built if not to keep invaders out or animals in?

It must be assumed that the walls did serve some other function, be it practical or otherwise, and one possibility remains to be considered; that the layout of these stones was intended to function as a landscape sculpture rather than the more usual territorial boundaries of a genuine fort community. Early large-scale landscape artworks can be witnessed at many other sites in the British Isles, and the easiest way to explore the possible implications of this type of layout in the modern age is to study the site from the vantage point of the eagle. Doing so in this case uncovers a remarkable secret that appears to have lain hidden from the enquiring eyes of onlookers for thousands of years. The layout of the walls of Foel Drygarn bears a distinct resemblance to that of a human skull, the teeth provided by the incorporation of a natural rocky outcrop of jaw-like form.

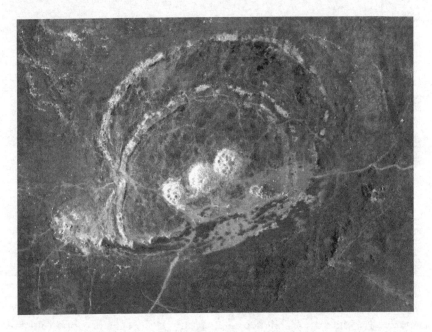

Aerial picture of the Skull of Foel Drygarn

If this was not a fort, what was its purpose, and why would it be fashioned into the shape of a skull? The bare and elevated nature of the hill has one distinct advantage; on a clear day it commands an unparalleled view of the area that stretches to the Lleyn Peninsula of Wales to the north, Ireland to the west and Cornwall to the south. Foel Drygarn, therefore, probably functioned as a place of observation at the very least.

As the most dominant feature of the site is the line of stone cairns in the centre, discovering the intended purpose for these most extraordinary mounds is likely to provide a key with which to unlock further details of its elusive past. Nothing has been found to suggest that the man-made stone hills were places where food was consumed, or bodies were buried, so they must have had some other, presumably very specific, purpose. It must be noted that their construction would have originally raised the height of the hill to equal that of the highest point on Carn Meini, and this practice was noted by E. T. Lewis, in his book, *Mynachlogddu: A Guide to its Antiquities*, as potentially linked with astronomical observation. Perhaps the cairns represent the three primary intellectual disciplines of early Preseli society, which is to say the brain within the skull.

Upon close inspection, the cairns reveal evidence of having once possessed hollowed out nooks in their lee sides, each large enough to accommodate a small group of people. After thousands of years of disuse it is not difficult determine that these recesses would have originally been larger and deeper, probably with vertical or terraced interior walls, before the inevitable process of collapse began to take place. Even today, the recesses offer a welcome refuge from the relentless winds of the summit. At one time, perhaps with the support of timber screens or roofing, these ancient hollows might have been used by a small or select group of people, to sit in contemplation of the surrounding vista.

The specific positioning of these hollows offers some support for the idea that the monument was a place of contemplation and observation. The most southerly cairn has a hollow that is perfectly aligned to look out through the 'eye of the skull' toward the Settlement at Carnalw, and even after the passage of several thousand years it is easy to discern that this particular view was deliberately celebrated and enhanced by the builders of the monument.

Looking out through the eye of the Skull to the settlement of Carnalw

A second depression in the same cairn faces two outlying peaks of the ridge that form the teeth of the skull, and the resultant line that runs between these peaks leads directly to the ancient burial site of Carn Meini, or 'Bedd Esus' as it is referred to here. It would appear from this initial appraisal that the Skull of Foel Drygarn was quite probably intended to represent the skull of the person buried on Carn Meini, in some sense at least.

Several obvious questions are raised by these basic observations. Might this monument have been the location where the meetings of the great thinkers of ancient times took place, or perhaps where their knowledge would be passed on to the next generation? Could the three cairns have provided sanctuary-like retreats for the past masters of science, sociology and philosophy, to study the heavens, to contemplate the future of mankind, and to discover their place in the universe? The choice of location, the layout of the monument, and the associated alignments all appear to point to that conclusion. If this skull-like sculpture was indeed conceived as an icon of human intellectual attainment, then it presumably pointed to an important forefather of Preseli Consciousness, rather than a great king, as the person originally buried on Carn Meini.

In summary, it would be the council of the forefathers of the Druids, the great thinkers of the Ancient Celts whose new view of the universe emerged sometime around 3000 BC, who would have been the group most likely to frequent a place such as this. Foel Drygarn, then, may have been the location where the technologies and theologies that gave rise to the development of Stonehenge were first discussed. In consequence, this site has provided the inspiration for the design of the Esus Skull, now an icon of Preseli Consciousness in its own right.

If this is a Bronze Age site, as is generally believed, it would most likely have a history, theocratic or otherwise, that stretched back another two or three thousand years. However, it must also be considered that this site may not be Bronze Age at all, as the dating seems to be based on the belief that this was a hill fort, and, as we have seen, Foel Drygarn does not conform to the standard hill fort model.

The particular alignments already discussed confirm that there was a connection between Foel Drygarn and the surrounding Neolithic sites. Looking for similar alignments between this and other, supposedly older, sites, might therefore provide further possible clues to the significance of the 'Preseli Skull'.

The First and Last Preseli Triangle

It is abundantly apparent that the three cairns of Foel Drygarn have been constructed in a straight line, and it can therefore be determined that their alignment with another ancient site known as Carn Bica was quite intentional. Carn Bica consists of a natural rocky outcrop that has been augmented by its builders to create a single cairn with three hollows in its northern flank, in exactly the same style as the cairns of Foel Drygarn. The most noteworthy point about this alignment is that it creates an angle with the primary line of the Great North Axis, at Foel Drygarn, that is precisely the same as the angle created by the line that runs between Foel Drygarn and Quarley Hill. Potentially, therefore, we have two sides of a Preseli Triangle here, suggesting that there may be a third version of the triangle actually located amidst the hills, and that looking for further evidence of its existence might well prove fruitful.

Travellers approaching Foel Drygarn along the Primary Line of the Great North Axis will pass by two marker stones known as the Waun Lwyd Stones. These stones create a doorway that aligns directly with Carn Bica, and, just as predicted, plotting these three lines on a map reveals the outer perimeter of another perfect Preseli Triangle.

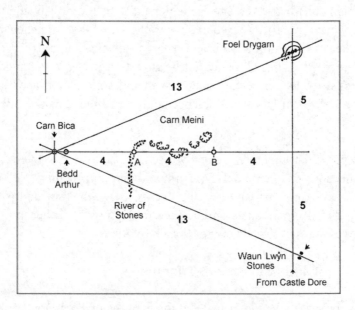

The Original Preseli Triangle of Wales

As this triangle encompasses the mount of Carn Meini, it has to be considered probable that this was the original Preseli Triangle, which, logically, would predate both the Giant Preseli Triangle and the Preseli Triangle of Stonehenge. This adds fuel to the argument that Foel Drygarn was built before the Bronze Age, or at least built on an earlier Neolithic site.

If evidence of the lateral line of this newly discovered ancient triangle could be found, the probability that these alignments are coincidental would have to be dismissed as infinitesimal. Lo! and behold, drawing in the eastward lateral line from Carn Bica takes us directly through the centre of the Bedd Arthur henge, and plotting the first Divine Point, precisely one third of the way along the central axis, finds the marker stone known as 'The Stone River Stone'. Not only does the alignment of this stone verify the existence of a Preseli Triangle within the hills themselves, but it also confirms that the Stone River is a significant, integral element of the ancient wisdom encoded within the monuments of the Preseli Cradle.

Note: It may be of some significance that while the first Divine Point, (Point 'A' on the above map) is celebrated in this Preseli Triangle, it is 'Point B' that is marked on the Giant Preseli Triangle by the Exmoor Complex. The Preseli Triangle of Stonehenge is the only version that celebrates both Divine Points, but it is, of course, possible that both points were originally marked in all three occurrences of the triangle. Sadly, many such marker stones have been taken by the farming community in relatively recent times, and used in the construction of buildings and walls.

Destiny and Chance

Reading:

Seus carving creates a personal truth: 3:7:7-11 (Page 89)
Creationism or Darwinism: 7:3:33-82 (Pages 190-194)
Humanity can fashion its own evolution: 7:4:23-41 (Pages 196-198)
The Stone Egg in the Age of Aquarius: 8:3:32-82 (Page190)

In *The Tome of Seus* 1:6:7 (Page 23) we are informed that the Druids
believed that "Destiny and Chance are the parents of the future."
This 'alleged' elementary Druidic truth may at first seem rather
simplistic, but what is particularly unusual about the statement is that
it applies the yin-yang concept to the unfolding nature of that which
is yet to be, and the principle can be applied to many different
scenarios. Later in the story, after the belief is confirmed as a
personal truth by the protagonist, it is applied to the concept of
evolution. From the specific and currently accepted perspective of
Darwinian theory, evolution is dependent upon chance, while the
component of destiny, or Creationism as it might be thought of, is
denied. So which of these two perceptions is correct?

As the alleged Druidic wisdom is portrayed as a universal truth, it
would clearly be worthwhile looking at the development process of
the individual human life, in order to gain a greater insight into the
nature of any parallels that may exist with the development of the

species as a whole. This idea is particularly relevant here, as the yin-yang union model has already been proposed as being the conceptual principle behind the Preseli Triangle. Further specific evidence that the Ancient Britons identified a distinct parallel between the male-female union and a higher universal evolutionary process will be considered later, but for now the focus will remain on the question of human evolution.

Since the time of Darwin, modern science has unravelled more of the picture of the human past and so we might now consider that the component of destiny is confirmed, manifest in the form of deoxyribonucleic acid, or DNA as it is more commonly known. Everything from the colour of our hair to the nature of our personality is affected by the random selection of genetic building blocks taken from a predetermined range within the universal structure of DNA. Therefore, while the outcome of who mates with whom, or which particular sperm wins the race in any one case, is governed by the chaotic process of chance, the necessity for that selection to be made from a limited, given set of genetic codes shows that destiny also has a hand in the shaping of an individual. What we also observe here is that the conception of an individual takes place in an instant of a yin-yang process, fertilisation. From this point on, the individual develops, mentally and physically, in a gradual process that is moulded by its environment. Were it necessary to determine the nature of this process from the evidence of palaeontology alone, we would surely be as mystified by the suddenness of the appearance of a new life as we currently are by the abrupt appearance of a new species in the fossil record. If the Druidic proposal is correct, the conception and development of the species would simply follow the same basic pattern that it does for an individual, so now we surely must ask the question; could the principle of 'Destiny and Chance' hold the key to the mystery of the evolution of the species?

Perhaps the most potentially revealing initial question of this investigation would be; does DNA have an evolution of its own?

74

DNA does not actually hold the plan of all life forms on Earth, for the genetic instructions for some viruses are provided by ribonucleic acid, commonly known as RNA. Many scientists subscribe to the 'RNA World Hypothesis' which proposes that life began in an RNA-only world and that DNA developed from there, principally because pre-cellular life would not have been capable of utilising the DNA structure.

It is conceivable, perhaps even probable, that the DNA code lay compressed within the similarly complex RNA structure, or more likely its predecessor, but that it could not be unfolded until a suitable non-biological, or pre-biological, living entity had evolved to utilise it. In consequence it can be determined that, while life on this planet has evolved from the simplest imaginable pre-cellular organisms, its evolution was enabled by the unexplained provision of a complex molecular structure that contained an essential, purposeful and highly developed 'Big Code' that was quietly waiting to be unfolded. While life in all its diverse complexity may have subsequently evolved from the most humble of beginnings, the ultimate blueprint for that development was clearly present in all its remarkable glory from the very beginning. The DNA code therefore, at least as far as the experience of this planet contests, did not evolve but was gifted to Earth in an already highly developed state, as a major part of the Big Code, or the predecessor to RNA and DNA.

At this point we are confronted by the long-standing argument of Creationism versus Evolution. Many Creationists argue that, as there is no missing link, evolution simply did not happen. Evolutionists on the other hand point out that evidence of design is purely speculative without proof of a designer. And so it would appear that, as the Creationists and the Neo-Darwinists continue to battle it out in the arena of modern science, both are wielding valid arguments, but neither is entirely right and neither is entirely wrong.

There is a simple question that we can ask that places the 'evolution versus creation' controversy into a sensible perspective. When

Humanity arrived on Earth, did they suddenly appear ready made, or did they develop from a pre-existing life form? Unless we are prepared to accept the idea that God waved his magic wand or despatched a species-carrying chariot to Earth each and every time a new species appeared, we have to accept that some form of evolutionary process exists, even if we can't work out what that process is. All we can say is that from the available evidence it seems logical to assume that there was a designer, AND, that one species evolved from another.

We can choose to view this apparent conundrum as a battlefront that will forever rattle back and forth between the two opposing parties, or as a fundamental starting point for the development of a new hypothesis. What we are directed to consider by the philosophy of *The Tome of Seus* is that there is a place for both the creationist and the evolutionist perspectives in the scheme of things; that 'Destiny and Chance', therefore, are indeed the parents of the future. However, while this sweeping observation might satisfy the philosophers amongst us, the devil is always in the detail for scientists, and just how this principle might play out in practice remains a mystery to be resolved.

Nowhere has the subject of the nature of evolution been more intensely researched and debated than in the world of the 'Dinosaur Detectives'. Dr. Gary Parker, a one-time evolutionist, wrote an extremely enlightening appraisal of the debate in his book entitled *Creation: The Facts of Life*. In his journey from evolutionist to creationist, Parker considered the specific case of Archaeopteryx, the classic example of a 'missing link' that supposedly shows how dinosaurs, or reptiles, evolved into birds. However, Dr. Gary Parker went on to systematically dispel the missing link claim, a view that he himself once supported, as a modern myth. In the following paragraphs, taken from his book, Parker draws our attention to some of the specific claims for a missing link that, on closer inspection, do not actually stand up to rudimentary logical criticism.

Is there any clue as to how legs evolved into wings? No, none at all. When we find wings as fossils, we find completely developed, fully functional wings. That's true of Archaeopteryx, and it's also true of the flying insects, flying reptiles (pterodactyls), and the flying mammals (bats).

Is there any clue in Archaeopteryx as to how reptilian scales evolved into feathers? No, none at all. When we find feathers as fossils, we find fully developed and functional feathers. Feathers are quite complex structures, with little hooks and eyelets for zippering and unzippering them. Archaeopteryx not only had complete and complex feathers, but feathers of several different types! As a matter of fact, it had the asymmetric feather characteristic of strong fliers.

While the evolutionists still profess that the missing links must have existed, and have actually dared to name some of the alleged species, even Yale's John Ostrom, one of the most eminent of their ranks, has been forced to concede that no fossil evidence has ever been discovered to support the evolutionist view. Parker deduces from this that the creationist perspective must therefore be correct, and summarises his evidence as follows:

As far as the fossil evidence is concerned, different kinds of invertebrates and plants have always been different kinds of invertebrates and plants . . . and birds have always been birds. The fossil evidence of creation is just as clear in the other vertebrate groups as well. It seems to me that "creation" is clearly the logical inference from our scientific knowledge of fossils.

An alternative concept called 'Punctuated Equilibrium' has actually existed for some time. This hypothesis falls on the side of creationism by proposing that evolution happens in big jumps, as opposed to the gradual Darwinian-type process. In the Nineteen Seventies, Stephen Gould of Harvard University attempted to re-

77

establish the idea, referring to the assumed species prototypes as 'Hopeful Monsters'. Unfortunately for Gould the idea was not well received, primarily because it failed to address some very fundamental issues. In his book, Dr. Parker sets out the failings of the theory in a concise and logical fashion.

> The hopeful-monster idea (variously expressed as punctuated equilibrium, saltatory evolution, or quantum speciation) was proposed to explain why the links required by gradual evolution have never been found. But the "big jumpers" were never able to explain how these big jumps could occur genetically, nor could they answer this crucial question about the first appearance of any hopeful-monster: *with what would it mate*?

> The "rear-guard" neo-Darwinian evolutionists like to point out the apparent absurdity of hopeful-monster evolution and claim that *evolution could not happen fast*. The punctuational evolutionists point to genetic limits and the fossil evidence to show that *evolution did not happen slowly*.

The Tome of Seus hypothesises that there is a second creational element of the evolutionary process, which is largely in accordance with the Hopeful Monster theory, but which differs significantly in that its success is reliant upon an interdependent partnership with a Darwinian style process of gradual change. The rudiments of the supposed evidence for this theory are presented in *Chapter VII*, the tale of *The Stone Egg*, this being the story of an archaeologist who discovered a fossilised dinosaur egg with a difference. At the time it was believed that dinosaurs did not have feathers, but the fossilised creature in this particular dinosaur egg did have feathers. The archaeologist apparently placed the egg on a shelf and forgot about it for a considerable number of years, because he simply did not understand what it was that he had found at that time.

This story is probably based in truth, with the egg having been one of many archaeological specimens that resided on the shelves of John

78

Ostram, the primary exponent of the revival of the 'bird to dinosaur' hypothesis of 1997, who began to re-examine some of his existing collection when reports of evidence of feathered dinosaurs began to emerge from China in that same year. Whatever the source, the story both expands and complements a previously discussed example of the case of human evolution, to provide a wider, more intriguing avenue of possibility for the process of evolution. Together, these ideas take the 'Hopeful Monster' hypothesis to another level, by explaining in rudimentary terms how the early 'human monsters' managed to mate, and showing how evolution can actually happen both quickly and slowly at the same time! The principle of this extended explanation is also outlined in *Chapter Seven*, in *The Old Story*, and the hypothesis is briefly outlined below.

Through this alternative process, many years in the past, we had a male and a female ape give birth to a human! At first, the ape community rejected the seemingly inferior human, but gradually more and more of these humans were born into the world, and eventually, a chance came when two of them were able to mate.

Because this process would have taken place over many thousands of years, it would be difficult to observe, retrospectively or otherwise, but evidence for this process may actually exist, some of which will be discussed shortly. The inference is that the DNA program is actually wired to make occasional 'deliberate' random mistakes when assembling the genetic building blocks for an individual of any species. This is not an entirely new idea, but here it is proposed that, given sufficient time, all of the possible combinations of hopeful monsters will be explored, and the opportunity for the fittest of them to mate will actually be realised at some point. We are reminded here of another of the simple wisdoms of the book, "In an infinite universe, if it is possible, then it will be".

Creationists argue that the Darwinian process has no effect upon evolution because it simply alters the balance of specific traits in a species, rather than altering its genetic makeup. For example, a farmer might successfully breed fat pigs, but they will always be pigs. More importantly, even if the 'fat gene' eventually becomes true-breeding in a population of fat pigs, they will be fat pigs that thin pigs can still breed with. They remain one species.

However, in the scenario that is being considered here, this does not mean that selection cannot have a bearing on evolution. The refining process of the Darwinian principle ensures that, when the next species leap finally takes place, the range of basic building blocks from which the 'deliberate mistake' will be made has been predetermined by the process of selection, natural or otherwise. Human DNA is actually a cut down, or refined, version of the greater DNA code. Consequently, Darwinian development, when considered in combination with its 'destiny' partner, provides a perfect explanation for how this DNA refinement process might take place within the greater process of evolution.

When the 'deliberate' mistake combines with the 'random' nature of the problematic gene selection, the theory once again reiterates that Destiny and Chance are the parents of the future. In a more fundamental echo of the same yin-yang principle, the new beings would continue to evolve, or be 'refined', over many generations, in accordance with a Darwinian style process, but the essential physiological leap would always take place within a single generation. Furthermore, with no apparent gradation process between the developed ape and the primitive human, there would be no missing link, and it certainly seems increasingly apparent as time goes by that this is precisely the case. There are no missing links. Perhaps the most likely fossilised evidence for such a process that we might find in the future would be to discover evidence of a bird within the egg of a dinosaur not known to bear feathers. Was the story of The Stone Egg also a prediction, we might wonder?

There is a simple message in *The Tome of Seus* for the scientists of today, who struggle to pass beyond the seemingly insurmountable stumbling block of the missing link. The answer will not be found in

Creationism, nor will it be found in Darwinism, because the answer lies in both, working together in a perfect and exquisite harmony.

The Destiny of Humanity

In *The Tome of Seus,* 7:4:23-41 (Page 196-198) it is said that humanity is unique because it has the ability to write its own destiny. Interestingly, this introduces a 'Creationist' component into the Darwinian element of the newly proposed yin-yang process of evolution, affecting how we as a species might evolve in a changing environment, in between the big leaps. Because we are now consciously aware of our ability to alter our environment, and our evolution is affected by environmental changes, we are potentially capable of plotting our own evolutionary path. Humans, therefore, could actually design their own destiny, in a way that is entirely separate from the recent technologically based genetic engineering processes of the laboratory. The implications of maintaining the current course, in which we are changing our environment without thought for the long-term consequences for our evolutionary path, are not good.

One of the chief areas in which our ill-considered choices are likely to have a detrimental effect upon our survival prospects is in the use of our ever-developing health systems. For example, each time medical science saves a prematurely born child it also makes a contribution to the creation of an environment where premature babies have an equal chance of survival to the fittest. This is in complete contrast to the process of natural selection, which ensures that prematurely born people don't reproduce, effectively setting course for a world where an increasing incidence of premature births eventually becomes problematic for society. Humans clearly make their decisions from the perspective of the individual, rather than from the perspective of the group, and the end result is that we are systematically engineering our own species to be dependent upon a technology that we may not always be able to provide. While this may be good for the individual now, it may well spell disaster for the

81

species in years to come, particularly as it is being applied in combination with so many other equally ill-considered processes. Alternatively, it might be considered that we are simply and unwittingly engineering our own cull!

In the Western world, those women who are naturally unable to conceive are now expecting scientific processes to provide them with children, creating offspring that will be all the more likely to be infertile themselves. So whilst farmers have always kept the largest pig to breed from, and humans have occasionally applied similar selective breeding techniques to themselves, they are more often using environmental controls to sustain an ever-weakening race. Extrapolating the effects of this current philosophy, even by just a few centuries, paints a very dismal picture for the future of humanity. In relative terms, the world will 'soon' be full of people who cannot conceive without the aid of medical science, who have prematurely born offspring that cannot survive without medical intervention, and who are physiologically dependent on complex drugs to overcome the major ailments that they are genetically predisposed to be born with. When this path is considered in terms of the longer periods that Darwinian evolution is normally associated with, the likelihood of a major disaster occurring in the 'near' future becomes obvious.

In our present society, survival of the individual takes great precedence over survival of the species, even though this potentially catastrophic imbalance of priorities defies the very logic that the human brain boasts. In the societies of other animals, particularly those of bees and ants, it is the survival of the species that takes priority over that of the individual, and, in this sense, the elementary logic of these humble creatures puts human society to shame. Evidently, selection of the 'selfish gene' is not a prerequisite of the evolutionary process, and destiny cannot therefore be called upon to supply an excuse for our current reckless path. Neither is this plain failing of ours something that can be blamed on the chance of Darwinian development, because the forward thinking society that gave us Stonehenge demonstrated that humankind can put society first, and implement long-term plans, perhaps most effectively achieved through the medium of education. The eventual downfall of the socially advanced Celtic Nation was not brought about by any want of a sustainable ethos, but by the forced intrusion of a selfish and greedy Roman culture with principles that were not greatly dissimilar to our own.

Sadly, such short-sighted policies as those under consideration here can and do affect other areas where humans exercise a tangible degree of control over their environment. Global warming is now with us, and already causing huge problems. Just a few decades ago, our politicians were actively encouraging the excessive consumption of the world's resources, whilst labelling the people who warned of the logical outcome of their reckless policies misfits and doom-mongers. Now, many politicians are proclaiming this truth themselves, but actually doing little or nothing to slow down the relentless and inevitable drive toward a catastrophe in the making, to which the vast majority of their policies continue to subscribe.

These observations compel us to confront a number of uncomfortable but now highly pressing questions. What can we do to reverse the destructive trends brought about by our terrible failings? Even if humanity could devise a system of government capable of leading us away from the precipice of doom, how could the current political hierarchies of the globe be persuaded to implement it? Is total annihilation inevitable? While it is the intention of this author ultimately to address these burning questions, for now the quest to lay bare the final secrets of the 'Destiny and Chance' relationship will remain the focus of attention. However, before moving on to the next chapter, it would seem an appropriate point to throw one more extraordinary idea relating to evolution, from the 'book of inspiration', into the bubbling mix.

In *Chapter Seven,* 7:4:33-41 (Page 197) when the protagonist Seus says "Think like the tree and eventually you will become like the tree" he draws our attention to the fact that we should also consider our spiritual or intellectual environment, as well as our physical environment, when contemplating the possibilities of the conscious planning of our own destiny, and to do this we must focus our plans on a time thousands of years hence. "The tree does not take life to feed itself, nor does it strike back when you cut it down". If humanity can learn the simple lessons that the tree already knows, it will acquire the opportunity to renew its lease on the journey of life, a journey that it has thus far successfully trodden for 600 million years. It now becomes apparent that, for humanity to survive beyond these difficult times, it must once again become a forward-thinking species.

The Mildren

Reading:

The Mildren: 8:6:20-31 (Page 232)

The Next Phase

An acceptance, cautious or otherwise, of the principle that Destiny and Chance are the parents of the future, finally allows us to pass beyond the irksome stumbling block of the missing link and dare to cast a constructive eye toward the image of the future. Now, as the first tantalising flashes of a New Age vision begin to shimmer in the distance, like a long awaited oasis on the horizon of human consciousness, we are duly compelled to ask the question, what does the future actually hold in store for us?

The Tome of Seus does not disappoint in its provision of a guiding light in this regard, as in *Chapter VIII* 8:6:18, we are reminded that one extremely effective way to see into the future is to look into the past, and, particularly, to identify an observed universal principle that might be applied to the respective issue. The book then goes on to apply that reasoning, speculating that, as from ape to man, there is another leap of destiny to be made on the road of our evolution, and it names the future offspring of humanity 'The Mildren'.

85

The accepted Christian, Creationist view of this issue is that God created humanity in his own image, and therefore humanity represents both the beginning and also the end of the road. In opposition to this narrow vision, in *The Tome of Seus* 7:3:60 (Page 192) we are once again directed to consider our future in terms of our own evolution.

> "It is quite arrogant of us to assume that we have arrived at the pinnacle of evolution," declared Seus. "That we alone are like Duw [God] and no other life form could possibly be on the same journey."

Not only are we advised here that humanity treads one of many paths in a complex exploratory process involving all forms of mortal life, but that we as humans are not the end product of our particular evolutionary drive. So what comes next we might ask? Who are the Mildren?

At this juncture we might choose to apply another of the alleged Druidic universal parallels of the book, the concept of The Fertile Age, in order to peer into the future and begin to tentatively draw in the details of our destiny. Just as the life span of the individual seems fashioned to incorporate a fertile period, sandwiched between its periods of growth and decline, so might the life of the species. If this middle phase of the process, humanity entering its fertile age, is destined to coincide with the dawn of the Age of Aquarius, as *The Tome of Seus* intimates, and evolution does happen both quickly and slowly at the same time, then we might expect to find some sort of evidence to show that the process of species transition has already begun! Are the Mildren actually upon us therefore?

Although it has been suggested that such a process would be difficult to observe in practice, because of the timescale over which the transition would take place, knowing what it is that we are looking for means that we have a much better chance of witnessing the process in action. So, in the tradition of the approach of the book in question, we will make use of another more simplistic life parallel to guide us on our way, dubbed 'The Chicken and the Soft Egg' by this author.

When a chicken enters the laying period, its fertile age, it begins to lay 'practice eggs'. These eggs will exhibit some of the qualities of the fully formed eggs of the mature hen, but not all of them. Generally these eggs will be lacking in one or more qualities. They may be misshapen, possess ill-formed shells. They may contain a part-formed yolk, or be all albumen, but eggs laid during the onset of the fertile stage of the hen will never be quite fit for purpose.

Now, recalling the evidence of the last great leap, from Ape to Human, we are finally ready to look for evidence of the children of the next transitional period within our current society, the soft eggs of humanity, so to speak.

Ape to Man

The first humans would not simply have looked different from their ape ancestors; they would also have behaved differently, because they were more intelligent. As the leap between the species involved a significant advancement in intellectual capacity, as well as the obvious physical changes, it might be speculated that the offspring of humanity will demonstrate similar traits. The chart below breaks down each of the two primary categories of change, Physical and Intellectual, into three distinct component parts, in order that their relationships can be explored for clues to the nature of the anticipated changes of the next predicted phase of evolution.

Intellectual Transformations	Physical Transformations
|	|
Logic Memory Imagination	Skin & Hair Brain Vocal Chords

On the intellectual side, the ability of the species to interpret the environment in a rational way underwent a giant leap in the transition from ape to human, with the new capacity for logical thinking providing a basic building block for the achievement of modern science and technology. However, such advances would not have been possible without a corresponding development in the ability to visualise the outcome of intricate theoretical scenarios, and then to remember those ideas and build upon them in a progressive way. While some apes are thought to be capable of achieving a vocabulary of about two hundred words, the average human is expected to master a vocabulary of ten thousand words between the ages of six and fourteen.

Therefore, the processes of the maturing of the imagination, which facilitated unprecedented creative advancements, and the enhancement of memory capacity, which provided a means with which to catalogue and recall observations and ideas, were also essential requirements of the great intellectual leap from Ape to Human.

Interestingly, it can be demonstrated that the intellectual developments did not function entirely independently of their complementary physical transformations. While the changes that affected our basic appearance, such as skin and hair, may be considered essentially superficial, the developments of the physical brain and the gift of superior vocal chords made a huge contribution to the human advancement.

Clearly, the intellectual developments would have been pointless without the accompaniment of a new brain, with sufficient processing capacity to allow all three aspects of logic, imagination and memory to flourish simultaneously and in relative comfort. Equally, without the development of advanced vocal chords, humans would not have been able to use their other gifts to develop language, which provided us with our greatest single tool for communication and the accumulation of knowledge. Without our advantaged vocal chords, it is unlikely that we would ever have developed the immensely valuable process of reading and writing.

Therefore, it was the intellectual advances in combination with the physical developments that facilitated the giant leap forward in our ancestors' ability to question and comprehend the workings of the universe, and so gave humanity the many blessings of that awesome new power of reason. The very fact that this particular subject can be written about and discussed provides pertinent testimony to this case. While it is impossible to imagine that our ape ancestors could have predicted the arrival of their successors, the superior intellect that separates human beings from the apes allows us that privilege of speculating rationally about the future.

If history is to repeat itself, and mankind is to give rise to the 'Mildren', advances in memory, creative and logical thought processes will almost certainly take another step forward, and, presumably, eventually be accompanied by some kind of critical physical development. In such circumstances, as with the transition from ape, an advancement of the size, or computing capacity of the brain would be likely, in order to accommodate the new-found superior intellectual capabilities.

Similarly, superficial physical transformations of some kind would be likely, less hair and smoother skin perhaps, but, we might ask, what kind of physical development could possibly parallel the acquisition of the all-important vocal chords of the earlier transition from ape to man? One possibility that immediately springs to mind is that of a sensory development, which would lead to some form of improved sixth sense perception.

It has long been accepted by many of us that the phenomenon of telepathy is real. Whales are mammals, like us, and they already use an encoded ultrasonic waveform communication system that is very much akin to the principle upon which telepathic communication is thought to operate. Humans have been shown by science to emit a number of types of brain waves, some of which we can learn to control when presented with rudimentary graphical feedback representations. However, our ability to consciously receive and evaluate those waveforms unaided is either generally very poor, or arguably non-existent. It could even be that the continuous development of non-telepathic communication systems, from the dawn of language right through to the advent of satellites, is responsible for a corresponding 'Darwinian' decline in our ability to process extra-sensory information. If we did at one time possess perceptible telepathic skills, the modern world of electronic communications, with it super efficiency and massive overloading of the airwaves, would certainly have struck an environmental deathblow to the need for those abilities.

Before moving on from the subject of extra sensory perception, it might be worthwhile considering the phenomenon of 'remote viewing', or the ability of some people to 'see' images of people, places and objects that are geographically far removed from their own location. The most famous instances are those of "Stargate", a US-funded military intelligence project that boasted some remarkable results. These included the discovery of a new class of submarine, being secretly developed by the Soviet military, and the pinpointing of the location of one of their bombers, which had been lost in Africa. The project was eventually abandoned shortly after its jurisdiction was transferred to the CIA in 1995, and following a retrospective evaluation of the overall results by the American Institutes for Research. The AIR ruled that the existence of ESP out of body experiences remained unproven by the project results.

It is the contention of this author that these remote viewing experiences do not actually occur 'out of the body' at all. Rather, it is perhaps more rational to consider that they are examples of telepathy, where the viewer makes a connection with the mind or visual memory of another person who has a real connection with the remote location. Had the American Institutes for Research concentrated their efforts on looking for evidence of telepathic

90

communication, rather than evidence of out of body experiences, the Stargate project might still be in operation today.

So, while we might speculate that the Mildren will look a little different, perhaps with dowsing receptacles to complement their advanced telepathic sensitivity, these ruminations offer little practical help in identifying evidence of a transition that might already be in process but as yet incomplete.

The intellectual advances in combination, even without an accompanying physical development, would certainly result in a child of the future, or the first of the Mildren, so to speak. But it must be remembered that we are looking for evidence of a process that will be happening both quickly and slowly at the same time, as outlined in the Destiny and Chance hypothesis of the Ape to Human scenario already discussed. So, thinking in terms of steps rather than leaps, we might ask; what might we expect to witness in an individual if just one of these intellectual steps had been taken, and was presented manifest within the confines of an otherwise human set of attributes? Let us now have a look at the three categories of development under consideration, starting with logical thought, and make our speculations one at a time.

Logic Development

What would we expect from an individual whose intellectual abilities in the area of the application of pure logic was highly developed but their super-logic processing ability was forced to work within the constraints imposed by the average human brain?

We might expect to see a person who was capable of performing tremendous mathematical calculations, but who was incapable of relating these calculations to their environment, or of applying them to their understanding of the universe. Maths is often said to be the pure science. It can't do anything in isolation; it doesn't mean anything on its own.

Memory Development

Time now to move on to the consideration of the likely traits of someone with a super-memory. In such an individual, whose brain was primarily devoted to the retention of information in isolation from any other complementary intellectual abilities, we might discover a person with a phenomenal ability to recall details, but who was incapable of putting their extraordinary talents to any great practical use.

Imagination

In the final case we will consider the anticipated character of an individual with a highly developed imagination, but whose talent is constrained by a correspondingly reduced set of complementary intellectual capabilities. Here we might expect to see someone who excelled in one or more of the arts, but who had difficulty in relating their creative abilities to the real world in an expressible way.

Who then might these people be? Do they actually exist in our current society?

The Soft Eggs of Humanity

People who fit these descriptions do already exist in our society, and they are generally identified as possessing the condition known as Autism, or one of the rare and highly specific branches of the condition that are associated with extraordinary skills in either mathematics, memory or art.

It now becomes obligatory to ask; are some people who are autistic, or perhaps all people who are autistic, the soft eggs of humanity? Can they say, "I have one of three intellectual conditions; I am a Mildren Being and I am a Human Being"?

Finally the time has arrived to attempt to place the 'Destiny' element of the principle of the Ape-to-Human scenario, already considered in the previous chapter, into a harmonious relationship with its partner 'Chance'. One day, perhaps thousands of years from now, a person will be born with an unusually well developed brain, a 'hopeful monster' if you will, who will also have one of these rare intellectual gifts. They may look quite different from the rest of us, smaller and weaker perhaps, with less hair. This time the gift will not be a hindrance, because of their unusually large brain capacity, and they will be able to make use of their special gift. Humanity may reject that child, but in time another will be born, and then another. Eventually an opportunity will present itself for these beings to mate, perhaps a memory child with a creative child, and so it will come to pass that the Mildren will inherit the Earth.

But will they?

Our Responsibility

The realisation that the Mildren may well be on their way immediately begs the question; should we make some form of preparation for their ultimate arrival? Sedine, a principal character in the *The Tome of Seus*, asks the final question in this regard. "Do we need to prepare for the Mildren?" The answer to her question is provided by Seus in 8:6:29 – 31 (P232)

"As it is the duty of parents to prepare a fitting home for their children, so it is the obligation of men and women to prepare the globe for the children of humanity," replied Seus.

"And if we don't?" enquired Beldou.

"If we fail in this duty, we will be cast into the cauldron of the cosmos and all signs of our existence will be obliterated by the hands of time."

93

So there we have it. Once again we are being asked to re-tune our perspective on the future to a far greater timeline period than we are currently used to considering. When the Mayans created their calendar, they gave us an end-date that lay thousands of years ahead. Now that end-date is upon us, yet we have lost our ability to see in such vast terms. Nothing is built to last. Even our collective political ambitions have a focus that is set little beyond the here and now. Concepts that require the consideration of the far future are only deliberated by scientists, and then only within the context of their own specific disciplines.

However, the application of a rational, philosophically driven and holistic approach to consideration of the future of life on this planet is finally re-emerging in the modern era, and the rediscovery of Preseli Consciousness will hopefully make an important contribution to that long-awaited process.

D4=R

Reading:

Gravity: 1:6:15-23 (Pages 23-24) & 2:2:28-59 (Pages 42-44)
The Expanding Universe: 3:2:23-45 (Pages 71-72)
The Hands of the Universe: 4:6:6-37 (Pages 113-115)

The Root of the Science

The radical approach to learning of the Ancient Celts, evidenced in their many and various extraordinary achievements, may well have been sparked by the philosophical musings of one extraordinary individual. However, their wisdom would have ultimately been accrued over thousands of years, after countless millions of hours of application of that early enlightened attitude by a long succession of their thinking élite.

If Foel Drygarn was indeed a centre of learning and debate we must surely wonder what the shamans of old would have discussed during their sessions on the mount. When envisioning such a meeting of minds, perhaps huddled together on the night of a new moon, with the vast and glorious heavens laid out above them and the humble fires of their tiny village flickering in the valley below, one can't help thinking that their science would have been philosophically driven.

In an earlier chapter we learned that *The Tome of Seus* asserts that the Ancient Celts had learned to view the Earth from the sky, and the subsequently noted archaeological evidence of their knowledge of the curved nature of the Earth certainly supports that contention. The logical end conclusion to be drawn from such an observation is that the world is spherical, and so it seems probable that the Ancient Celts of Britain had discovered that the Earth was itself a celestial body, which moved in a similar fashion to the other celestial bodies that they had studied so intently, thousands of years before Columbus began to consider the simple idea that the Earth was round.

If the Preseli people had observed that the universe was made up of celestial bodies that moved in a complex but orderly orbital dance, it is equally logical to assume that they had also contemplated the nature of the forces that hold that remarkable process in place, and in particular, had considered what the nature of gravity might be. What follows is an attempt to decode the theory of the principles of a ten dimensional physical universe, complete with a partial explanation for the mysterious force of gravity, presented within *The Tome of Seus* as having been hypothesised by the Ancient Celts. Whether this theory was actually developed in the days of antiquity and subsequently decoded from the layout of a monument like Stonehenge, or was received as channelled information by the author or authors of the book, or is simply the product of an anonymous modern mind is hard to say. Nevertheless, the hypothesis in itself is highly intriguing.

Gravity: a Key to the Visualisation of Universal Expansion

The explanation begins with the claim that the Earth is moving towards us all the time, hence the reason that we return to Earth rather than flying off into space when we jump into the air. This informs us that; the force of gravity is, at least in part, caused by the same force that we experience when we go up in an elevator. As long as the elevator is gaining, or losing speed, localised gravity will add

96

to, or subtract from, the fundamental effects of gravity, and we will feel heavier, or lighter.

Sedine, a character in the book, raises an apparent flaw in this theory when she points out that "people on the other side would fall off, because the globe would be moving away from them". Her point might seem to be supported by the fact that no one is ever to be found travelling on the underside of the floor of an elevator. However, the hypothesis counters her objection by claiming that gravity is a force associated with the expansion of the universe, a process rather like an explosion in which all the stars and planets are moving away from the centre of the universe but, because of our perception of time, the explosion is happening in a kind of super-slow motion. Put simply, gravity is caused by universal expansion in the fourth dimension of space. However, even though this theory sounds very simple, it is not a concept that is particularly easy to visualise, and naïve misunderstandings are possible.

In the course of writing his book: *Relativity, The Special and General Theory*, Einstein considered the concept of an expanding universe, as hypothesised by the Russian mathematician Friedmann, a proposal which was supported by the research of the famous astronomer Hubble who observed light rays 'apparently' bending as they passed close by the Sun.

Hubble's observation could be interpreted as evidence of the expansion of the universe, or alternatively, as evidence of light being bent by the force of the sun's gravity. To understand the first scenario, consider a beam of light setting out for the surface of the sun from a distant star many light years away. However, by the time the beam arrived, the sun would have grown. Therefore, the beam of light would actually strike the sun, rather than skimming its surface. To an observer of the process on Earth, like Hubble, the beam of light would appear to have curved in to strike the body of the sun, rather than having maintained its original direct course for the surface. The greater the size of the heavenly body in question, the

97

greater the degree of apparent distortion of the path of the light would be.

However, in the alternative view of Einstein, the most obvious explanation for the apparent curving of a light beam, as it passed by a celestial body like our sun, would be the influence of gravity.

To decide which of the two theories was correct, Einstein used Hubble's calculated rate of expansion to work backwards, to determine the date at which the expansion process supposedly began, or how old the universe was. If the results tallied with the estimates of conventional wisdom, then the probability would be that the universe was indeed expanding. However, Einstein went on to dismiss the theory of expansion because, based on a single measurement made by Hubble, he calculated that the 'Big Bang' occurred only 10 to the power of 9 years ago, which is far too short a time.

What Einstein failed to consider was that gravity might be, at least in part, a by-product of universal expansion, (where the Earth and the sun are expanding within a similarly expanding universe) in which case the rate of expansion would have to be accelerating for gravity to exist. We experience the effects of this principle every time that we go up in an elevator, as we only get that feeling of heaviness when the elevator is accelerating upwards. As soon as the elevator speed becomes constant, our weight returns to normal. Had Einstein used two measurements, separated by a gap of several years, he would have arrived at an entirely different conclusion, and perhaps *The Tome of Seus* would never have been written.

The scientists of today accept the idea of Friedmann, that the universe is expanding, but the hypothesis considered here implies something quite extraordinary about the nature of that expansion, which does not yet seem to have been considered by conventional science. The explanation continues by suggesting that, if this process of expansion was applicable to all matter, including structures like the atom, our planet and everything on it would be continually growing, but because the process would be relatively slow, in our perception of time, and everything around us would be growing at the same rate, (including the rulers with which we make our measurements) we would be unable to detect the changes. The only consequence of the expanding universe that we would expect to detect would be the effect of gravity, which we do! Of course, if such a scenario was a reality, observers like Hubble would also see light appear to bend as it passed by large heavenly objects. This strange concept of the nature of universal expansion will be considered again in *Chapter VII*, in relation to the perception of the relativity of time, the concept of infinity and the nature of matter, but for now we will concentrate our attention on the implications of the new theory, with respect to multiple dimensions.

Friedmann's determination about the expanding universe came as the result of his remarkable, primary mathematical discovery, that the universe should be ten-dimensional. In our recent past, before Columbus, we perceived the surface of the world to be flat, or two-dimensional, so our perception of the world was essentially three dimensional, with two dimensions of space and one of time. Consequently it was believed by seafarers that the world actually had an end, inhabited by strange and dangerous monsters, and that venturing indefinitely in any one direction would ultimately result in disaster. Since that time our perception of the universe has been transformed, by the integration of the notion of a third dimension of space, which is nothing more complicated than the concept of up-and-down!

In the new system, the rules of the two-dimensional Earth still held good for the journeys of the old seafarers, but now we can use the newly discovered third dimension of height to define positions that take the curvature of the Earth into account, and to plan our journeys out into space.

Scientists have subsequently speculated that there might be another dimension of space, and more recently, they have become convinced that an elusive fourth dimension of space actually exists, somewhere. However, while the consequent explanations for its whereabouts have been many, including unworkable geometric 'tesseracts' and impossibly complex mathematical formulas, they have all fallen a long way short of the beautiful simplicity of the 'up-and-down' dimension of the 'Columbus' breakthrough. So far, these variously complicated ideas have tended to describe the universe as being folded up, usually in some exceedingly convoluted fashion. However, they all fail in the simple sense that the explanations can always be accommodated within the three simple dimensions of space that we already know about. Consequently it can confidently be stated that, however clever these ideas might appear to us less technically minded mortals, none of them offers a true explanation for the fourth dimension of space.

By contrast, *The Tome of Seus* claims that, to fully appreciate its explanation for gravity being a by-product of universal expansion, we have to learn to 'see' the universe in five dimensions, four dimensions of space and one of time, and it then proceeds to teach us just how to do it!

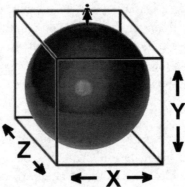

According to this idea, the fourth dimension consists of nothing so romantic as a tesseract or hypercube, and nothing so complex as a mathematically compressed dimension. The solution is really a very simple concept indeed. To begin the explanation we will first consider the notion of the three-dimensional universe that most people are already familiar with.

In the image on page 100, the Earth is represented by a sphere. Any point on the Earth (the location of the little lady for example) can be described by use of coordinates marked off along the X, Y and Z axes, which correspond to the three known dimensions of space. In this scenario, if the Earth was growing, or expanding, the rulers that we have set along these three axes would also be growing at the same rate. Therefore, according to the dimensions set out along these rulers, the position of the lady would remain the same, and the expansion of the Earth would not therefore be detectable.

Now consider that the sphere above represents our universe. Any point within the universe (the centre of the Earth for example, or a lady stood at the edge of the universe) can be specified by employment of the same coordinates X, Y and Z, which still correspond to the same three known dimensions of space.

It is time now to imagine that the universe depicted above is expanding, and that rather than seeing a snapshot of that process, from a specific moment in time, we are actually watching the little lady and everything in the universe slowly expanding. Try to visualise the universe in your hand, about the size of a pool ball, with the little lady standing at the top. Now imagine that you can watch that process of expansion for just one minute, and in that minute the universe and the lady both gradually double in size. The final position of the lady would obviously have changed by the end of that minute. In short, by the end of the minute, the lady would have moved out a little further into the space. Would we, as observers of that process, be able to specify the new position of the lady by using the same three rulers? Although the lady has grown, and moved, so have the rulers that we would use to measure her. The answer to the question is clearly an emphatic no. According to those rulers, she

101

would be in precisely the same position, but we know that she has moved!

Therefore, to define a point within an expanding universe, we would require the familiar coordinates of X, Y and Z, plus one other; the radius of the universe at the time that we wished to plot the position.

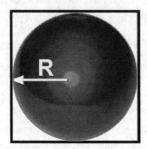

It now seems obvious that, to define a point in an expanding universe, four dimensions are required: X, Y, Z and R, where R is the radius of the universe at the time that the definition is made. In this new system, the rules of the old static three dimensional universe still hold good, but now we can use the fourth dimension of R, to define a position which takes the expansion process into account; just as the third dimension of space allowed us to take the curvature of the Earth into account.

According to this hypothesis then, the fourth dimension of space does not lie in some garbled origami-like illusion, nor is it folded up in accordance with a lengthy and unfathomable mathematical formula. The fourth dimension is simply another basic parameter of space, like length, width and height. The fourth dimension of space is, therefore, an ever-rising number that we must multiply our conventional measurements by when we wish to consider our universe in terms of five dimensions. The fourth dimension of space in our universe is simply its radius.

$$D4=R$$

Long may the expansion of R continue, for without it there would be no order, no gravity and no life.

Friedmann's Mathematical Model

At this point the eager student might be compelled to ask, what of the other five dimensions predicted by Friedmann? Does the hypothesis under consideration here offer us an explanation for the whereabouts of these even more elusive realms of measure? Rest assured, the hypothesis does not disappoint. Once again, the answer is yes!

Imagine for a moment that we already live in a ten-dimensional universe, and that the tesseracts of recent theorists are now banished to the realms of hyperspace, along with the monsters that once terrorised brave seafarers daring to approach the periphery of the flat earth. The universe is now seen as a five-dimensional entity, but as we peer inquisitively around the new beast, in search of the other lost dimensions, we see absolutely nothing. But, if we are prepared to learn from one of the metaphors of nature, as our greater holistic hypothesis so frequently advises, we will find that a possible answer to this puzzling question is quite literally within our grasp. The fingers on our hands that we first learn to count with may just offer us a clue to the infuriating riddle of the lost dimensions.

If the universe were split into two halves, each containing five dimensions, there would be four dimensions of space and one of time in each half. *The Tome of Seus* describes the 'Big Bang' as "the last time that the two hands of the universe came together, in a mighty and thunderous clap". Just like our hands therefore, which have four fingers and a thumb, we could expect the right hand to be a mirror of the left. According to the hypothesis, in the case of the universe this reversal takes place in the fourth dimension of space. Therefore, we have not been able to find the other hand of our universe because, until now, we have not been able to visualise the fourth dimension of space. It seems that our problem has been that we have only had one

103

hand with which to clap, but thanks to the hypothesis under consideration here, now we have two. Theories speculating as to the whereabouts of the other hand of our universe might soon be many, but what follows is the preferred explanation of this author.

In order to attempt to locate our right hand, we must transport ourselves back in time, to the moment just before our universe started to expand, and assign to the point at its precise centre the value zero for each of the dimensions x, y, z, r and t. Now this point, which we have just defined with pinpoint accuracy, represents the time and place where our two hands last met, perhaps in a mighty and thunderous clap, and from there on, our half of the universe began to expand. Now we must ask ourselves; where did the right hand go after this?

If, as we assume, the right hand is a reversal of the left in the fourth dimension, we can surmise that the right hand would begin to contract in an opposite fashion to the left. Therefore, today, as this book is being written, the other half of our universe would appear as a super-dense antihole situated at the now familiar coordinates $x = 0$, $y = 0$, $z = 0$, $r = 0$, $t = 2011$ AD. Such an antihole would possess a phenomenal antigravity, exactly equal and opposite to that of the visible universe, which, until now, we have considered to be the entire universe.

Within this tiny almost unimaginable place would reside the lost dimensions: -x, -y, -z, -r and -t.

The Fertile Age in Stone

Reading:

The Cards of Time: 1:1:27-38 (Pages 6-7)
Christianity, Gnosticism and The Eternal Soul: 4:5:6-25 (Pages 109-111) &
8:8:44-45 (Page 239)

Stonehenge

The notion of the 'Fertile Age' has been considered briefly in earlier chapters, with respect to four entities, or realities, or, we might even say, four scales or aspects of living reality. These are the journey of the individual and the journey of the species, the journey of the mortal soul and the journey of life itself, and, in an all-encompassing sense, the potentially life-sustaining period between the birth and death phases of the physical universe. By definition, then, the notion of the Fertile Age can be viewed as one of the universal parallels of the Preseli Consciousness, which together, acting like keys of wisdom, allow us to access the principles behind numerous seemingly-disparate fields of study in a holistic and therefore enlightening way. So the time has arrived for us to place the master key of the Fertile Age into yet another lock, in an effort to resolve one of the greatest mysteries of our time; to consider the ultimate significance of the Preseli Triangle, and to uncover thereby the prime intention and purpose of the monument known to us as Stonehenge.

To make a start in this quest we will return briefly to the homelands of our truth-seeking predecessors, and, more specifically, to the great skull of Preseli. If Foel Drygarn is a sculpture of the skull of a Celtic Deity, the significance of which is only revealed when the monument is considered in aerial view, the possibility must be acknowledged that other monuments built by the same people may have had similar symbolic messages encoded into their ground plans. Even if this was not the case, the ground plan of any purposefully-man-made structure must contain meaning, and the aerial view may well show what that meaning is. Stonehenge has been studied from this perspective before, but, being a complex structure consisting of many separate parts, the exact primary purpose has so far eluded all who have ventured to cast an analytical eye towards its multiplexity. Accordingly, it is only now, when the existence within it of the Preseli Triangle has finally been revealed, and, indeed, that this triangle is a primary component of its design, that we can turn attention away from the many soli-lunar features of Stonehenge and so analyse and interpret the layout at this even more fundamental level.

Stonehenge has long been known for its alignment to the midsummer and midwinter solstices, and there is a general consensus amongst archaeologists that some form of ritualistic event would have taken place annually in times gone by at Stonehenge on one, or perhaps both, of these occasions. Such an event would have involved some form of symbolic procession, perhaps made by shamans, or, perchance, by royalty, along the dominant northeastern avenue that leads through various doorways to the heart of the monument; and a most remarkable parallel is revealed when the newly discovered essential Stonehenge layout and its associated summer solstice ritual are reconsidered from an aerial vantage point. The passage of the processionary party along the path of the midsummer sunrise into Stonehenge, perhaps with the chief participant carrying some kind of token offering, strongly resembles the passage of the sperm as it arrives to fertilise the egg.

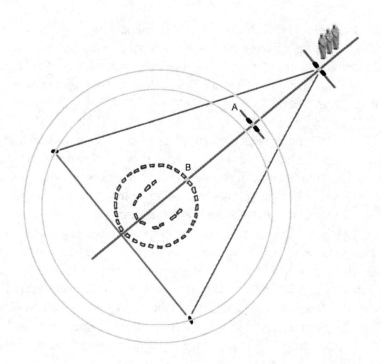

Fundamental Stonehenge layout

As the processionary party arrives at the first point of significance, the tip of the Preseli Triangle, or the Heel Stone entrance, it might be considered symbolic of the sperm entering the female form, through the vagina. Of course, all this also prefigures, and harmonises with, what has come down to us, despite the opposition of the Roman Church, as the natural religion of Wicca.

Continuing along the processionary route, the offering would pass next through the first Divine Point (Point A, or the Slaughter Stone entrance). It seems not by chance that this point coincides with the outer perimeter of the Stonehenge circle, which is here representative of the outer wall of the egg. The penetration of the egg by the sperm would certainly have been an event worthy of special note in such a ceremony, surpassed only by the divine union between the sperm head (the male nucleus) and the female nucleus at the second Divine

107

Point (Point B). This final event would presumably be symbolised by the passing of the offering through the entrance to the Sarsen Circle, which provides a truly grand representation of the nucleus of the egg, and a wholly fitting place for the final celebration of the creation of embodied earth-life.

So what of the rest of the stones at Stonehenge, so many of which are quite obviously placed to mark the passage of time? Why would the study of the movements of the sun and the moon be appropriate at such a monument, if its primary dedication was to terrestrial fertility alone? The answer to this apparent quandary is immediate and simple. Stonehenge was designed to celebrate something more than astronomical change per se, and also something greater than the conception of new human life. The building of Stonehenge was a colossal engineering project that took well over a thousand years to reach its intended completeness. Quite possibly, therefore, the monument was conceived as a tool to measure the temporal progress of the Fertile Age of the whole universe, as its builders were, without doubt, extremely forward thinkers.

In this more universal parallel between heavenly observation and earthly life, the entry of the ceremonial offering at the tip of the triangle would represent the first spark of life entering the physical universe at the onset of its Fertile Age. This process would occur along the line that divides the left and right hands, as represented by the upper and lower halves of the Preseli Triangle, thus combining a fundamental graphic representation of the biological reproductive process with a highly durable calendar. In doing so the Ancient Celts were demonstrating their grasp of a significant parallel between the fertility processes of organic life on this planet and, in a far greater sense, the grand birth, life and rebirth process of the universe itself.

The essential belief that "In the beginning there was the egg and the seed" is clearly supported by this appraisal, but in the universal representation there appears to be a twist. In this scenario, the universe consists of an alliance between the yin element of the Outer

108

Circle and the yang element of the Preseli Triangle. Here, life is instigated at the appropriate moment of maturity through the introduction of a third element, the 'spark of life', which, like the sperm, is represented by the offering of the ceremony. In the human representation, the spark of life is already present within the mother and the father, but in the universal representation this is not the case. The universe, as we think of it, would not have been able to support that spark of life until it had reached its Fertile Age. The grand scale of the monument serves to emphasise the point that our attention is being directed beyond the human experience to a time and place far greater than the here-and-now. Where exactly this mysterious spark of life might have originated, if not from within the physical universe, will be considered in the following chapter, but, for now, we will continue our appraisal of the more immediate of the two depictions.

At Stonehenge, the human representation is predominantly focused on the journey of the sperm to the ovum, the yang element in the reproductive process, with no discernible representation of the ovaries, the fallopian tubes or the uterus visible in its ground plan. This omission might be passed off as due to emphasis having been placed on universal fertility rather than on the human anatomy. However, the 'yang' perspective is further stressed by the representation of the various processes in mathematical and geometric terms, which are essentially applicable to a yang perception of the physical universe. If the builders of Stonehenge were intent on incorporating a statement about the yin-yang nature of the universe into so splendid a monument it seems unlikely that they would then take the ill-considered decision to create a disharmonious balance between their yin and yang representations, unless, of course, the yin perspective was to be symbolised elsewhere, in a second, separate monument.

The River of Stones in the triangle of the Preseli Cradle, with its original Bluestone circle at its head, may have represented the universal sperm, while Stonehenge represented the egg, with a third yet-to-be-identified monument providing the final piece of the metaphorical jigsaw puzzle, the great biological cauldron. This third monument may also represent, as we have now intimated, the womb not merely of embodied life-forms but of the whole universe.

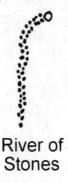

River of Stones

Where, then, is the postulated yin partner of Stonehenge? If no such monument could be found it would be perfectly rational to accept one of the following explanations; that the builders of Stonehenge failed in their undertaking to construct a counterpart yin monument, that the yin monument is now lost, or that the idea that Stonehenge is a part of a representation of the universal laws of fertility is simply wrong.

The Yin Mother

Casting an enquiring eye across the Wessex landscape in search of a potential sister monument for Stonehenge soon locates the magnificent circle of Avebury, the only other monument of fitting scale and complexity in Southern Britain. The Avebury complex is of such huge proportions that it actually dwarfs its suggested partner, and it boasts a most extraordinary feature known as Silbury Hill. Constructed from around a million tons of meticulously crafted and flawlessly assembled giant blocks of chalk, which were then covered over by earth, Silbury Hill must have been of enormous importance to its builders, but its purpose has, thus far, eluded the archaeologists of the modern era.

Having been built between 2700 and 2200 years BC, Avebury is of the era of Stonehenge, and therefore a part of the collective consciousness of the builders of both monuments. Although the first phase of Stonehenge, now recognised as having been completed in Bluestone, would have pre-dated Avebury by some 300 years or more, Avebury would almost certainly have been completed before the final phase of Stonehenge. This makes them fully contemporary with each other, and, since they are just seventeen miles apart, implies that their design and construction were authorised and financed under the jurisdiction of a common, extremely powerful and forward-looking authority. Therefore, if Stonehenge does have a yin partner, Avebury is the only realistic contender; but does Avebury fit the necessary yin profile?

In their book, *The Wessex Astrum*, Peter Knight and Toni Perrott offer a most apt and enlightening description of Avebury:

> The megaliths themselves are like an open art gallery – horses, human-like heads, vulva cavities, phalluses and other fantastic imagery leap out of timeless stone, inviting us into the world of the prehistoric shaman, a world of imagination and ancestors. We see this as one of the main differences between Avebury and Stonehenge. The latter is engineered, the stones are cut and crafted, the monument seeps masculine science and engineering. At Avebury the stones are uncut; it is a shamanic landscape.

So Avebury clearly exhibits the essential yin profile which, in turn, lends considerable credibility to the presumption that a universal yin-yang partnership was deliberately created between the two monuments. Even so, nothing less than hard evidence of a dedication to yin fertility, of equal significance to the already-declared yang symbolism of Stonehenge, would be required for confirmation of this hypothesis. Now an obvious and quietly smouldering question regarding this idea suddenly assumes a patently fervent glow; does the groundplan of this remarkable monument, as at Stonehenge, provide a visually encoded indication of its ceremonial purpose?

111

The first person to consider this question was the famous 18th Century antiquarian, reverend and doctor, William Stukeley. In his time the monument at Avebury was in a far better state of repair than it is today, and Stukeley was able to produce a reconstruction of the monument in the form of a drawing the authenticity of which is still accepted by the scholars of today.

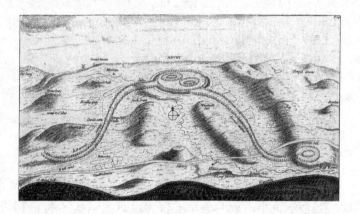

Stukeley's detailed drawing of Avebury

Stukeley's plan clearly depicts two avenues, wending their way in mirror-image fashion from the immense central henge of the monument down through the natural valleys of the east and west flanks, each terminating on a seemingly convenient plateau below. To the uninitiated eye the Stukeley plan is fundamentally symmetrical in design. One is therefore immediately drawn to the conclusion that, originally, a stone circle must have existed on the plateau to the west, which was intended to be the complement of the circle that, in Stukeley's time, was still evident on the plateau to the east. However, if evidence of a western circle existed in Stukeley's time, he did not find it. Instead, he saw in the monument a symbol that he believed was fully present and complete in the reconstruction as he depicted it, and in consequence of that conclusion he called a prompt halt to his archaeological investigations. However, we have reason, while respecting his survey and depiction, to consider it incomplete.

112

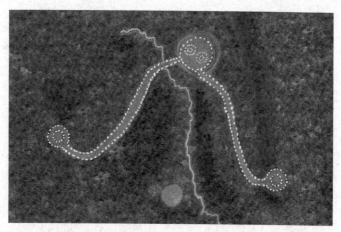

Artist's aerial view of the whole Avebury complex

Note: This reconstruction is, of course, somewhat conjectural, but reference has been made to the modern Ordnance Survey map, to available aerial views of the present-day site, and, especially, to Stukeley's perspective drawing. The reconstructed view is as accurate as it can be made using these sources.

In the book *The New View Over Atlantis* John Michell explains the process that led Stukeley to his conclusion regarding the landscape symbolism at Avebury.

> For some time Stukeley had been curious about a certain quality in the prehistoric landscape, an elusive meaning behind the arrangement of stone circles and earthworks. At several places he had noticed in the groundplans of these monuments certain recurrent forms – the serpent and the winged circle – which he identified as the symbols of the former patriarchal religion, on which Christianity itself was constructed. At Avebury this intuition was confirmed, for here, stretched over several miles of the landscape, and perfectly shaped in structures of earth and stone, he perceived the twin symbols of alchemic fusion, the serpent passing through the circle.

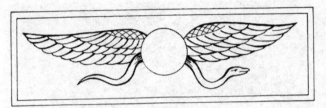

Stukeley's reproduction of the Egyptian Winged Serpent

Stukeley observed a distinct similarity between the layout of Avebury and a symbol of a winged serpent that he, a founding member of the Egyptian Society and an avid Egyptologist, was already very familiar with. But the vital element of the serpent image is a masculine symbol, and totally at odds with the now-accepted view of Avebury as a divinely feminine Goddess Temple. What is of perhaps even greater concern in this regard is the glaringly incomplete nature of the design as Stukeley conceived it. If this really was a representation of the Egyptian symbol, surely the wings would be an important feature of the Avebury design, and, for builders who achieved so extraordinarily complex a monument, no more difficult to represent in stone than was a serpent. So where are the wings? While there is a possibility that some kind of remote symbolic connection between the Avebury layout and the Egyptian design might actually exist, Stukeley's conclusion is, unfortunately, far from confirmed even by his own drawing.

What, then, was the layout of this monument actually intended to represent, if not the winged serpent of Egypt? If we now return to our initial instinctive reaction to Stukeley's reconstruction, and assume that there must once have been a circle on the western plateau, we might begin to reconsider this fascinating question in an entirely new light. Unhappily for the antiquarians of our age, the temptation to produce their landscape drawings in accordance with conventions that apply only in modern map-making sometimes proves a handicap. When interpreting a Neolithic landscape it is frequently necessary to remember that the orientation of the design is not bound to conform to our frequent practice of placing the vertical axis of any drawn plan along a North-South line. Unless the intended

114

structure was dictated by astronomical considerations, its orientation is far more likely to have been determined by the topology and, perhaps, seen by the Neolithic builders as already part-realised by nature.

So now, with the assumed western circle at Avebury reinstated into Stukeley's plan, if we simply rotate the picture through 180 degrees, an entirely different, and wholly appropriate, interpretation becomes possible. Stukeley did not draw an image of a serpent passing through a winged circle. He produced a highly accurate but slightly incomplete diagram, albeit upside down, of the female reproductive system!

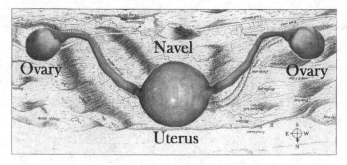

The Female Reproductive System

Unlike Stonehenge, where the focus of attention is placed on the journey of the sperm, the ceremony here will have been oriented toward the journey of the egg, as it passes from the ovary, along the fallopian tube and on towards the uterus.

It can be deduced from the presence of the two egg-like circles constructed within the great uterus that there would have been two processionary parties at Avebury, each presumably setting off from the smaller east and west circles simultaneously, and each in possession of an appropriate symbol of fertility. In the lesser sense, these eggs, once fertilised in ceremony, would perhaps represent the male and female, the Adam and Eve of the species, whilst in the greatest sense they would represent the yin and yang of a living universe in the making. In view of the enormous size of the

115

monument, it would have been necessary for the entire event to be orchestrated from a single vantage point, presumably by a female shaman, and so the mysterious purpose of Silbury Hill is also suddenly revealed. This strange, indeed unique, structure, plainly now the navel of the monument, was a perfectly designed and painstakingly crafted podium from which the annual ritual celebration of feminine fertility was both conducted and observed. And what a ceremony it must have been to behold!

Confirmation of the intended purpose of the one monument is clearly to be found in the complementary nature of the design of the other, and so the suspicions of the more intuitive of those who have dared to speculate about the nature of these two great sites have been confirmed; Stonehenge does indeed relate to masculine science, and Avebury is without doubt a Goddess Temple. Now their true joint purpose is also laid bare for all to see. Stonehenge was constructed to celebrate the yang element of fertility, whilst Avebury was designed to celebrate the yin. Betwixt the two, we have evidence that the Ancient Celts possessed a deep and holistic understanding of the concept of fertility, comprehending both a detailed expression of the workings of the human biological reproductive process and a remarkably perceptive grasp of the mechanisms of the physical universe.

Editor's Note: It was not only in the East that the notion of a unity expressible as "As Above, so Below" arose. The unified view of Preseli Consciousness that we postulate here pre-dated by at least a millennium Hermeticism, Platonism, Neo-Platonism and Pythagoreanism, and, before them, even the Vedic and Upanishadic systems of India.

A Homage to Stukeley and Blake

Stukeley has often been ridiculed by the scholars of later times, not so much for his interpretation of the Avebury stone formation but for his belief that the monuments of the Neolithic and Bronze Ages were associated with the wisdom and practice of the Druids. What this document suggests is that Stukeley and Blake were, in all essentials, perfectly correct.

116

At this point it would perhaps be appropriate to remind ourselves that the wisdom of the Druids could not have been born instantaneously out of the air. Such profound knowledge would have had an evolution, a story of accumulation that stretched far back into the past. The incompleteness of the archaeological remains and the lack of written records create the entirely false impression that the Neolithic and Bronze Ages were distinct periods, with two entirely distinct civilisations, but they were not. The very terms 'Neolithic Age' and 'Bronze Age' are labels invented in our own era, and totally alien to the peoples concerned.

If used without imaginative empathy, these terms cause us to neglect the continuities in the rest of the society's life. Humans made discoveries and inventions, but they did so without disrupting its historical flow. In Western Britain, the development of metallurgy was a gradual process experienced by a race of people who lived in relative peace for an enormously impressive period of time. Just as their knowledge of mining and smelting techniques would have been developed gradually, and passed on from one generation to the next, so would their knowledge of science, engineering, geometry, astronomy, biology and philosophy. Nothing would have happened quickly. There would have been no distinct dividing lines between the ages.

The so-called historic and pre-historic eras are, similarly, frequently viewed as virtually separate entities, but, again, the usage is seriously misleading. Therefore, the latter, scantily documented phase of Druid history must have possessed a highly cherished pool of accumulated intellectual advancements, which had been developed in a process that tracked the common progress of the stable society of which the Druids and their predecessors formed a part. Even through times of great wars our own society has managed to maintain and build upon its considerable intellectual base, much of which is founded on ancient knowledge, and to pass its accrued wisdom to the next generation. Why on earth would we think that the Ancient Britons would be any different? This book likewise is both a demonstration and a celebration of that same process, for it builds on the work of Stukeley and Blake, and the more recent work of pioneers like E. T. Lewis, Robin Heath and John Michell, and, particularly here, on the significant contributions of others whose names remain undisclosed. These people, in their turn, have all built on the remnants of the ancient wisdoms that they have found secreted in the landscape. These wisdoms were instigated long ago, in the Preseli Hills, source of the Bluestones and birthplace of the philosophy that eventually gave us Avebury and Stonehenge.

It is now perhaps appropriate to ask; might there be, after all, some truth worthy of investigation concealed within the image of the serpent? Stukeley believed that the winged serpent was a symbolic depiction of the Holy Trinity, the circle representing God, the snake signifying the Messiah, and the wings a symbol of the Holy Ghost. He interpreted the model of the Holy Trinity as being a pre-Christian, Druidic concept, and, even though he was a Christian himself, he believed that Druid philosophy had given rise to the Christian faith. He also deduced, by simple logic, that the origins of the symbol lay not in Egypt, but in Britain. In the following passage from *The New View Over Atlantis*, John Michell explains the connection.

> Stukeley, a profound Bible scholar, widely acquainted with the literature of antiquity through his studies in Latin, Greek and Hebrew, considered Avebury in terms of comparative religion, as a monument of the old true faith, whose holy citadel had been founded in Britain. The tradition from which Stukeley drew his conclusions was one whose origins are said to coincide with the first moment of human enlightenment, a tradition based on constantly renewed revelation and codified through the ages by philosophical schools all over the world. It illuminated the work of the Pythagoreans, the Platonists and the medieval transcendental magicians, and was preserved above all among the Hebrew cabalists and the Gnostics of the Christian Church.

118

This was a view that Stukeley would certainly have discussed and developed with his friend William Blake, whose belief in the holy citadel was so famously expressed in his poem 'Jerusalem'.

Copy of Blake's interpretation of The Holy Trinity

In the depiction of the Holy Trinity to be found on *Folio N105* of *The Notebook of Blake*, now in the possession of the British Library, Blake portrays an undeniably human father, finally reunited with his equally mortal son after the crucifixion. While these two people could only have been reunited in the spiritual world, it is blatantly apparent that Blake viewed them as having both once lived mortal lives. The Holy Spirit is suitably positioned above the depiction of the Father and the Son, signifying the anticipated eventuality of a third incarnation. The distinct similarity between Blake's portrayal of the Holy Spirit, equipped with wings and soaring through time towards its destiny, and Stukeley's winged circle, confirms that Blake, too, considered the concept of the Holy Trinity a construct inherited from pre-Christian times.

It is probably no coincidence that the notion of the Holy Trinity, perceived as a Druidic concept, is also referenced in *The Tome of*

119

Seus, the book that provided a guiding light for much of the research upon which this title is based.

The Trinity of Esus

The depiction of the Trinity, as presented in *The Tome of Seus*, utilises a triple metaphor, each of its three representations being symbolic of a specific aspect of the concept of a triune spirit. In essence, *The Triple Metaphor* stipulates that there were three incarnations of Esus, the first having been Esus the 'Father Spirit', an ordinary mortal man who lived before the building of Stonehenge, whose enlightenment and wisdom were celebrated by the Celts much as the followers of Buddha commemorate his history today. The second incarnation of this tale tracks three specific and notable days in the recorded life of Jesus, so it seems that, being metaphorical, the account is an interpretation of the Holy Trinity, with Jesus as the 'Son Spirit', the second incarnation of Esus.

According to this version of events, therefore, Jesus had two fathers; a mortal father who was a Druidic King and a spiritual father, his own earlier incarnation, who was Esus. We are thus presented with Esus the human Father, Esus the human-and-spiritual Son, and Esus the Spirit yet to be. As this involves reincarnations, the link to the philosophies of the East is unmistakeable. The similarity with the unorthodox symbolism of the 'Holy Trinity' as conceived by Blake is equally, or perhaps even more strongly, apparent.

The possibility that this idea is actually based on a discernible history is explored in the book *The Almighty King* by Einon Johns. A surprising amount of evidence is uncovered to substantiate the claim that Jesus was a mortal son of a mortal father who had many mansions in "the world above" and who was perceived by some as the awaited, and expected, reincarnation of the Celtic deity Esus. The biblical reference to the voice of Jesus as "the voice of many waters" is presented as partial evidence, that Jesus sought to extend his own philosophy with none but the shiniest pearls of wisdom that could be

120

offered by the greatest shamans of the known world at that time. Where else would Jesus have acquired his considered philosophy if not from discussion with the greatest shamans of his time, prior to the Judean experience, during the thirty years of his life about which the biblical record is blank?

Evidence that a bloodline connection once existed between the royal families of Judea and Britain is also revealed, and this provides considerable support for the greater case. In this interpretation, the world 'above' Judea and the Roman Empire would have been the distant and seemingly exotic world of the Celts, established long before Rome, and ruled by an almighty but benevolent Druidic overlord who was a real historical character, as opposed to an Almighty King in heaven who was not. We are reminded of the relevance of the words of an ancient Welsh manuscript, which states that Jesus was born in the time of Cymbelyn, the last of the great Druidic kings of Britain, and of many other gems of evidence revealed through several new translations made by Johns of other previously-overlooked ancient texts. This rationalisation of the historical, largely either biblical or non-canonical, gospel evidence, creates a case glaringly at odds with the highly implausible Romanised Christian account, which claims that Jesus was divine rather than human, and that he was spawned in a miraculous conception by a 'Father' who was God in Heaven.

It is clear from this detailed decoding of the religious allegory of *The Tome of Seus* that the book's author is, like Blake, implying that the 'Triune God of Christianity' is a misinterpretation of the earlier Druidic concept of a triple incarnation. There are references to such an idea even in the canonical Bible, specifically in *Chapter 19* of the *Gospel of Luke*, but we cannot digress to deal with these here. It is also claimed in *The Tome of Seus* that Stonehenge was built as a monument to the wise ancestors, principally to Esus, and would be a place where the days to his return would be counted by means of its astronomical calendar. This conflict between the doctrines of the Druids, both early and late, and Roman Christianity provides us with a plausible explanation for the demise of the Druidic Cult and the abandonment of Stonehenge at about the time of the arrival of Christianity in Britain, but is there any evidence to connect Jesus with the Druids?

According to a letter entitled *Epistolae ad Gregoriam Papam*, written to Pope Gregory by Saint Augustine in AD 600, the first church of Christ was set up by none other than Jesus himself, on an island in the western extremes of Britain. Gildas the Wise, a Celtic Priest of the Fifth Century, provides us with a date for this event of AD 37, placing Jesus in Britain four years after the alleged Resurrection. While some may consider these accounts unreliable, evidence does exist that the first Christians were shown favour by the British in those early years. From the point of view of this brief deliberation, it seems rational to believe that the Druids and the Celtic Christians shared much of their theology and enjoyed free access to sacred land sites held to be of great significance.

Adding to this case is the archaeological record, which also indicates that the transition between the two disciplines proceeded with a peaceful and organised fluency. The honouring of the sites and monuments of the Ancient Celts by the Celtic Christians, who so often chose to build their new Churches within the ancient stone circles erected by their predecessors, aptly demonstrates this process. Equally, many of the ancient menhirs of Cornwall and Wales were preserved and Christianised by the later Celts, while, by contrast, other such monuments were frequently smashed and used to build the houses and decorate the gardens of the later wave of Christians who came from Rome.

If Jesus was really associated with, or educated by, the Druids, we might hope to see some surviving evidence of this still present within the records of his teaching, despite the imperialistic campaign by Constantine's established Roman Church. From this perspective, The *Gospel of Thomas* might be considered a potentially revealing text, as it is essentially a Gnostic work and, having escaped the Roman purge of allegedly heretical gospels, did not suffer at the hands of the early church Councils. 'Gnosis' being a word, derived from the Greek, used of a special kind of 'knowledge' not revealed to or grasped by everyone who called himself Christian, we can understand why it was, from Thomas' point of view at least, what Jesus had said that was important, rather than what he had done. Thus we have here historical evidence in perfect keeping with the image of Jesus that emerges from the hypothesis now under consideration, for Thomas portrays Jesus as an ordinary mortal philosopher rather than as the superhuman miracle-man familiar to us from the four canonical gospels.

Analysis of the remaining portion of another Gnostic text, *The Gospel of Mary*, one of the now famous 'Nag Hammadi' transcripts that survived the imperialist advance by secretion in a desert cave, provides further support to the case. In her book *The Gospel of Mary of Magdala: Jesus and the First Woman Apostle*, Karen King makes the following appraisal of a recent translation of the ancient text.

> Both the content and the text's structure lead the reader inward toward the identity, power and freedom of the true self, the soul set free from the Powers of Matter and the fear of death.

This summary provides a remarkably pithy description of the concept of the Indestructible Soul, which is notable as one of the key aspects of Ancient Celtic theology. *The Gospel of Peter*, true author unknown, is yet another non-canonical text that provides particular evidence of a parallel between these same two, supposedly separate philosophical disciplines, the Druidic and the Celtic Christian. In *Paragraph Twelve* we learn of a surprising belief held by the author of the text.

> Some said, "Mary conceived by the Holy Spirit." They are in error. They do not know what they are saying. When did a woman ever conceive by a woman?

The author's belief that the Holy Spirit was female is in keeping with the yin and yang assessment derived from analysis of the layout of Stonehenge, where the physical half of the universe is the yang father, and the 'non-physical' half of the universe is the yin mother. Clearly, in the view of the writer of the *Gospel of Peter*, The Holy Spirit is a kind of universal Mother Spirit, and Jesus is the child of both a universal mother and a universal father, not of two mothers, an earthly one and an unearthly. However, while his perception of the Holy Trinity relates exclusively to this universal concept, he does accept the existence of a separate, mortal connotation of the Father and Son relationship. Soon after his denunciation of those who, as he sees the matter, fail to recognise the Holy Spirit as unable to fertilise a human female, the writer provides us with another astonishing revelation.

> And the Lord would not have said "My Father who is in Heaven" (Mt 16:17), unless he had had another father, but he would have said simply "My father".

So, in the eyes of the author of the *Gospel of Peter*, whatever the maternal genesis of Jesus, he had two fathers, one in heaven and another who was presumably mortal and resided on earth. As has already been noted, this is the view presented in Blake's drawing, and it is also specifically reiterated in *The Tome of Seus* and, furthermore, given considerable historical support by Einon Johns in *The Almighty King*. The Roman Christian Church would have us believe otherwise, and has gone to extraordinary and often violent lengths to eradicate all evidence of this once common, rational perception of Jesus.

The Triple Metaphor

In view of the increasingly apparent accuracy and depth of the symbolism present within the allegorical subtexts of *The Tome of Seus*, it now becomes evident that the representation of the concept of the Trinity encoded within its complex fictional frame might also be worthy of further consideration.

The Triple Metaphor of *The Tome of Seus* is illustrated by a pack of cards. When cut into three piles, the pack of cards can represent the past, the present and the future, eras that, more specifically, relate to the three timescales spanned by the book. The present is portrayed as the era of Jesus, at the point in the book when the metaphor is declared, the past being the time of Esus and the Ancient Celts, referred to in the book as the Deruu. The future is presented as the transitional end-period of the Piscean Age, leading to the dawn of the Age of Aquarius. These three time periods are of particular importance because they equate to the eras of the three alleged incarnations of Esus, the final incarnation being depicted as having occurred, in a physical sense, in an era that is actually now in the past.

The pack of cards, once shuffled, is also symbolic of the book itself, where the three timescales have all been jumbled up. Here, the protagonist is represented by a card called the 'Prince of Serenity' and it is noted that this card could now fall anywhere within the shuffled pack, thereby signifying that Esus may be represented in different timescales at different points in the book. The aphorism that "A story can contain many tales" is perhaps a further clue to the deeper, more elusive meaning of this second metaphor, as it draws a parallel with the way the many tales in the book comprise one greater tale. This exemplifies the way the many stories of individual souls combine to create the story of life itself, the evolution of mortal life on earth being a necessary companion to the unfolding story of the universal soul, or at least of Earth's chapter of this greater tale, and this deeper meaning gradually becomes apparent as the chapters of the book unfold.

The third and final meaning of the metaphor is far more difficult to discern, but a question that is raised by the protagonist, "Do I stay and risk death . . . or do I leave before my quest is complete?" draws

125

our attention to the crucial focus of the riddle, the three quests of Esus. At the moment the question was asked, soon after the alleged Resurrection (of Christ), the protagonist would have actually completed the second quest. Therefore, when he subsequently noticed that the cards had disappeared, he would have realised that the final quest was to be completed during the incarnation of the 'spirit yet to be', many years hence, and he would thus have had the answer to his question.

It is this concept of the three quests that bestows specific purpose upon the three incarnations of Esus, and it is the 'Third Quest' that is of the greatest relevance to us in the Age of Aquarius. The specific objectives of the three quests are to be considered in our final chapter, but their collective purpose, initiated six thousand or more years ago, is both elegantly simple and ambitiously grandiose, as it is to secure the salvation of life beyond the human phase, beyond the Fertile Age of our planet, and beyond the eventual destruction of the universe. While some might believe that such extreme forward thinking was beyond the reach of the Ancient Celts, the evidence in the stones is beginning to suggest otherwise.

The Ethereal Jewel

Reading:

The First Stonehenge: 1:4:30 (Page 15)
The Ethereal Jewel: 5:6:14-31 (Pages 138-140)
Greater and Lesser Universes and Time: 3:4:8-25 (Pages 80-82)
Infinity: 2:6:15-24 (Pages 57-58)

Universal Symbolism

In order to gain a greater insight into the symbolism of Stonehenge, and thus to progress this unfolding philosophy a little nearer to its conclusion, let us now attempt a reconstruction of the fundamental layout of Phase One of the monument. According to *The Tome of Seus* four-score Bluestones were used to build Stonehenge I. It has now been ascertained that fifty-six of these stones were set out in a circular arrangement, located in the holes now referred to as the 'Aubrey Holes' that lie just within the confines of the outer earthworks. Another nineteen stones have been determined as having been deployed in the inner circle of the final layout, and it might be logically supposed that these nineteen stones were a primary feature of the original plan, having been temporarily cleared from the site to allow work on the huge Sarsen circle to be carried out later. So now we have two stone circles, but, if we assume that the Preseli Triangle of the final monument was also a feature of the original design, five stones are missing, and we must put them back in place to define the true, original, complete outline. Interestingly, this makes eighty stones in all, four-score stones, just as the book states.

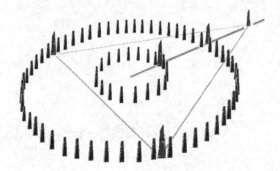

An artist's reconstruction of the first Bluestone-henge

While the basic symbolism of this underlying format has been given due attention from a human biological viewpoint, the greater holistic perspective has not yet been fully explored. Reducing the plan to its universal elements reveals two concentric circles and one triangle. The triangle has already been identified as representing the yang element of the universe, or the two hands of the physical universe, but what, if that is correct, does the mysterious yin element symbolise, and what shall we say of the inner circle?

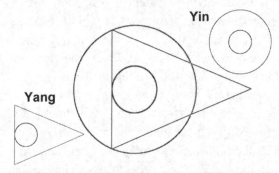

Stonehenge Yin-Yang Representation

In the universal yang representation, the central nucleus would be symbolic of the physical Earth, as the life-giving element of the material universe. In this sense it is clearly more analogous to a

128

'father' image than the more widely accepted view of a 'mother' planet. Yin and yang therefore, like us, are not exclusively male or female. When the initial chaos of the great creation process eventually settled to form the current array of planets and solar systems, the sheer scale of the cosmic arrangement would have raised the probability that one of these systems, at least, would possess the necessary physical characteristics to sustain life. This rational viewpoint reminds us once more that the hand of Destiny has been interlocked with the hand of Chance from the very outset of creation.

In this view the process is more analogous to the biology of the plant world than to that of the animal kingdom, for here it is the mysterious yin mother who holds the seed, complete with an embedded blueprint for all of her many offspring. As the fruit reaches maturity it falls toward the ground, where the yang ground, embracing the seed, supplies the physical requirements necessary for it to develop, according to its predetermined genetic plan. So, similarly, as the universe approached its Fertile Age, the yang planet had developed the physical attributes necessary to sustain the seed of life that had been simultaneously developing within its yin partner. Finally, in a remarkable marriage of the heavens, as when the flint meets the striker plate, the spark of life was released and the fire of evolution was kindled.

Now we see that the Earth is both our father, as the material aspect or component, and, correspondingly, simultaneously our mother supplying the energetic component. The Earth, as represented in the symbolism of the Stonehenge layout, would have been the product of the same two elements of yin and yang that Avebury and Stonehenge represent. While we already have a tremendously well-developed understanding of our physical universe, our understanding of the other mysterious elements of our inherited Neolithic geometric representations of the universe is extremely limited, and one of the necessary keys to the acquisition of this particular wisdom is a knowledge of ancient numerology.

Numerology, Infinity and Time

Mathematics is sometimes described as the pure science, since, of all the disciplines, it alone can stand unaided. Its truths are within itself. It needs no physical world to demonstrate them. When the numbers in a numerical sequence or a mathematical formula fall into perfect symmetry they create a glorious and magical truth of incomparable, primal beauty. The Ancient Celts, it seems, were aware of this. Their effort to correlate the movements of the sun and the moon with the passage of time shows their deep fascination with numerology, and signifies their belief that the universe functioned within one great cosmic law of number. How far beyond the spheres of sacred geometry, astronomical periods and universal representations their cosmic law of number was perceived as extending is not possible to say, but by the time of Plato both the intervals of music and the functions of human consciousness were being viewed as integral harmonics of this same magnificent rhythm.

These enduring principles of number, divined in an age when philosophical consideration and rational deliberation were the parents of progress, were all but abandoned in the modern era. While the remnants of the great achievements of the ancient scientific view of the universe still permeate our calendars and systems of measurement, their methodology has been disrespectfully daubed with the labels of witchcraft and magic. In more recent times, however, as scientists have finally begun to equate the problems of comprehension of the physical universe with their understanding of energy and particles of matter, the idea that the missing pieces of the puzzle might lie buried deep within the mathematics of Pythagorean symmetry has been resurrected.

Of course, we see from our studies of Stonehenge and the Preseli Triangle that Pythagoras, who was born some two and a half thousand years after Stonehenge was instigated, must have been informed, indirectly or otherwise, by the wisdom of the shamans of Ancient Britain. Likewise, the discovery that the units of measurement of the inner circle at Stonehenge were later adopted by some of the most accomplished cultures in the ancient world demonstrates that the wisdom of the Ancient Celts reached many of the greatest philosophers during the millennia that followed. So, let us now take an even closer look at the Preseli Triangle, to see what other clues to the ancient mystic science of number might remain secreted within its frame.

Prior to the publication of this book the Pythagorean lunar triangle, with its 5:12:13 proportions, had been noted as providing an exact analogy to the cyclic phases of the moon. The connection with the annual solar rhythms at Stonehenge, where two of these lunar triangles were arranged to form the Station Stone Rectangle, has also been recognised for some time. However, the proportions of the twin Pythagorean triangles of the Preseli Triangle, with its divine point situated one third the way along the dual axis of time, total to a related, but different, set of numbers: 8, 10, 24 and 26. It can be no coincidence that these are the very same numbers that the physicists of the modern era were so excited to discover as inherent in the quantum theory of hyperspace, although, outside of the mathematical world, they have managed to identify just four of the associated dimensions. It seems that modern science is only now beginning to discover what was quite possibly a long established ancient truth.

Study of the Stonehenge layout has already indicated that the Ancient Celts perceived our universe as having two dimensions of time (the numbers 8, 10, 24 and 26 being derived from the numbers 4, 5, 12 and 13, each multiplied by 2), and later we will learn, from further revelations in *The Tome of Seus*, that innumerable dimensions of time might exist. In the modern world, Einstein was the first scientist to realise that time was also a dimension (of a universal space-time continuum), and, as only three spatial dimensions had and have been identified by science, time was instantly labelled 'the fourth dimension'. Speculation about the existence of another dimension of space continued, but from that point onward the elusive fourth dimension of space was relegated, by its revised title of the

131

'fifth dimension', to a rather ill-considered position at the end of the list. While the 'fifth dimension' of *The Tome of Seus* has been revealed to us as a cause for gravity, through a philosophically driven visualisation of the expanding universe, for modern science the fifth dimension currently remains an unimaginable entity that can only be understood in terms of mathematics.

Often the mathematics behind a universal law will be discovered in advance of the physical principle to which it is eventually found to apply. It may come as no surprise that the next step in the development of the higher-dimensional thinking of the modern age was to be proposed by a mathematician, Theodr Kaluza of Germany. By positioning Einstein's theory of gravity within a five- rather than a four-dimensional mathematical model, Kaluza was able to integrate the theory with that of another great scientist, James Clerk Maxwell, who had argued that light consisted of vibrations in an elusive fifth dimension.

So, then, it seemed that the hand of science had at last four fingers and a thumb, although one of these metaphorical dimensions was still a purely mathematical construct, but, alas, the scientists still had but one hand with which to clap. Along came another mathematician, Alexander Friedmann, and the physicists were rescued for a second time. Friedmann's argument of 1922, already briefly discussed in *Chapter Five*, was based on a mathematical discovery in which he noted that the universe must have been continuously expanding, within a ten-dimensional structure, from its very inception. This theory was important because it raised the likelihood of the phenomenon of a 'Big Bang' for the first time. However, even though the argument was supported by the observations of the American astronomer Hubble, Einstein publicly rejected it, in the hastily written *Appendix IV* of his now famous book on relativity. This resulted in Friedmann's remarkable discovery being largely ignored by the scientific world for several decades.

It wasn't until the accidental rediscovery of an extraordinary notebook in 1976, penned by an unknown Indian Mystic and self-styled mathematician named Srinivasa Ramanujan, that Friedmann's revelations were to be afforded due respect. Unfortunately for the memory of the German mathematician, his ten-dimensional vision was immediately overshadowed again by the final disclosure of the Ramanujan theorems, which proposed that the universe had, in absolute total, no fewer than twenty-six dimensions.

Ramanujan was no ordinary man. He had little interest in material wealth, being purely motivated by an obsessive desire to discover and record the entire set of mathematical formulas of the laws of the universe. He was born into a poor family in 1887, near to Madras, but with such a phenomenal talent for mathematics that he would eventually come to be hailed a genius by the most distinguished members of the scientific community of the West. Sadly, he met an untimely death at the age of just 33, shortly after contracting tuberculosis, and the best of his remarkable mathematical accomplishments were to remain undisclosed for many years, secreted within 130 pages of scribbled notes in a box at Trinity College. The fact that he and he alone could visualise, compute and record the theorems of the complete multi-dimensional universe set him far apart from all his formally educated peers, who could only look upon the results of his work in awe and wonder.

However, Ramanujan was incapable of explaining how he had 'seen' his calculations, except to say that the answers had appeared to him in dreams. His ability to communicate the nature of his ideas to others was severely limited and, despite being rescued from relative poverty and brought to Britain by fellow mathematician Godfrey H. Hardy, he spent long and frequent periods hidden away in mental institutions. The profile of Ramanujan is one that we have considered before, as a forerunner of the next generation of humankind, in our chapter on the Mildren. This, then, is the profile of a Mild! Srinivasa Ramanujan was one of those rare people identified in this book as living evidence of the process of human evolution, and we failed to recognise the relevance of his life in these terms during his own time.

According to the impeccable symmetry of the seemingly divine calculations of the Indian genius, the universe actually conforms to a ten-dimensional model that, in turn, operates within an all-encompassing twenty-six-dimensional frame. If Ramanujan's formula is complete it is, of course, the same great cosmic law of number that the ancients laid out in their plan of Stonehenge so many thousands of years earlier. Of great significance in this case is the number twenty-four, largely because this number is to be constantly found popping up throughout the entire collection of the Ramanujan theorems, but also because it is a number that is closely associated with ancient numerology, and with the Preseli Triangle in particular. So, if the number of great importance to both Ramanujan and the Ancients is twenty-four, why has a twenty-six-dimensional universe been declared necessary by the physicists?

Just as with the ten-dimensional vision of the universe postulated here, where the eight dimensions of space are only complete when two further dimensions of time are added to them, so it is with the twenty-four-dimensional theorems of Ramanujan. Symmetry is only achieved when the number twenty-four is augmented to twenty-six. While the scientists can confidently declare that this increment is essential to maintain the symmetry of their various subsequent theories, in both the case of the number eight and that of the number twenty-four, they don't actually understand why.

From the perspective of the hypothesis of *The Tome of Seus* so far revealed, the answer to this riddle is almost solved. Discounting the dimensions of time for the moment, we have already identified the eight-dimensional physical yang element of our universe. Similarly, we have identified the universal yin partner, which we might reasonably presume is also an eight-dimensional entity. If we now look for inspiration to the 'triple eight' format of the ancient symbol revealed in *Chapter One*, we finally realise that the universe is neatly

134

composed of three eight-dimensional elements which are collectively accompanied by two further common dimensions of time. The mathematics for any one of these entities requires the addition of two dimensions to achieve symmetry, making ten dimensions in each case, while the universe as a whole, with twenty-four non-time dimensions in all, still only requires the addition of two dimensions to achieve a similarly perfect state of harmony.

$$8 + 8 + 8 + 2 = 26$$

The nature and function of this third eight-dimensional entity is yet to be considered, but for now the spotlight will remain on the still-unfolding history of conventional, accepted science. What the rediscovery of Ramanujan's book of theorems achieved, in practical terms, was to open the doors of Einstein's then languishing vision of the universe into an exciting new branch of physics called quantum string theory.

String theory asserts that the particles of matter that make up the universe are created by an array of incredibly small vibrating strings. As the strings vibrate, it is the patterns of movement that occur about their resonant points that creates the particles of matter that make up atoms. Just as the strings of the banjo sound different from the strings of a double bass, so it is with the quantum strings. The characteristics of each type of particle will vary in accordance with the differences between the lengths and types of the quantum strings. But, despite the idea of string theory having been established in the scientific world for several decades, physicists still don't actually have much of an idea about how it relates to the real world. In his book *Hyperspace*, Michio Kaku, one of the chief exponents of String Theory, freely admits that:

Physicists have not the slightest understanding of why ten and 26 dimensions are singled out as the dimension of the string. It's as though there is some kind of deep numerology being manifested in these functions that no one understands.

135

We are reminded here of the Ancients' extensive knowledge of universal numerology, which is increasingly being discovered reflected in the design of their greatest monuments. Kaku continues with his disclosure:

> When asked by audiences why nature might exist in ten dimensions, physicists are forced to answer, "We don't know".

With its theoretical particles being derived from various fundamental frequencies of vibration, string theory echoes the idea of the ancients of a universal law based on musical intervals of natural resonance. But before a layman like this author can be finally convinced of the truth of string theory he needs the answer to an obvious question, and it is almost needless to ask: From what is the string made?

Perhaps it is sometimes the function of the physicist to act like the wise priest, and to facilitate a marriage between the rationalised ruminations of the philosopher and the exquisitely elegant equations of the mathematician, particularly as the road of Preseli Consciousness, in this regard, appears to be clearly laid.

Time, Infinity and the Non-physical Universe

Now armed with an appreciation of the importance of number to the ancients, and an understanding of the value of mathematics in the current age, we are almost ready to ask the remaining question; could the concept of a non-physical component of the universe be seriously entertained within the court of modern science? In order to consider this question in the context of Preseli Consciousness, we must first attempt a seemingly impossible feat, and try to focus on infinity.

On page 58 of *The Tome of Seus*, when Seus ponders the possibility that the universe might be infinite, he is directed to consider the humble world of the ant.

"The ant could be forgiven for believing that the terrain upon which he walks has no end," said the Old Man, breaking the silence. "For the ant, a journey to the shores of this land would be unthinkable. As unimaginable as a journey to the outermost star would be for us." He paused to look at Seus. "But what lies beyond the shores of this land?"

Extrapolating the reasoning implied by the observation of the Old Man gives us the answer to the question with respect to the universe. Although it is not possible for us to journey to the edge of our universe we can deduce that the edge must exist. What, then, is infinity, we must wonder, and the Old Man has an answer for this question too.

"... to begin to contemplate the nature of infinity, you must consider the existence of another greater universe, beyond the shores of your own." His voice began to fade into the distance and Seus found it hard to see him. "And another beyond that . . . And another beyond that."

Later we are directed to consider that, equally, we should look inward towards infinity, and in doing so we discover that, as well as the concept of the 'Greater Universe', there is also the concept of the 'Lesser Universe' to be considered. This idea entails the necessity to view the passage of time in the greater and the lesser universes as progressing in accordance with their respective, individual harmonic codes. The people of Stonehenge measured their time, just as we do, in terms of orbits of the planet around the Sun, or years, as we call them. The phases of the moon and the yearly cycles of the seasons were all viewed as integral parts of the magnificent symphony of the universe. If we think of the analogy between our solar system and an atom as reflecting the concept of adjacent universes, then one orbit of an electron around its nucleus would be analogous to a year in the time of a lesser universe. Everything in this lesser universe would therefore happen at a lightning pace in the time of the greater universe. As *The Tome of Seus* puts it, "civilisations would come and go in the blinking of an eye". Time, we might therefore deduce, is relative!

From the observable parallel elements of our universe, atoms and solar systems, it might be noted that, while there are similarities between the structures and laws of these seemingly adjacent universes, one does not simply appear to be a perfectly scaled version of the other. We must therefore be aware that it is conceptual constructs that are being considered here, rather than strict, directly-comparable physical realities. There may or may not be atoms somewhere within our universe that have supported a Fertile Age, and the greater and lesser universes, should they exist, may ring to a symphony that is very different from that of our own.

However, in accordance with the rules of mathematics, it is perfectly possible to consider that our universe might be a component of another macro-universe. Equally, again from a mathematical perspective, it is possible that one of the atoms of our universe, or another one like it, might constitute a solar-system-equivalent in some other micro-universe, perhaps complete with life. Further to this conception it is credible, if also unprovable, that the atoms of that universe might, in their turn, be components of yet another micro-micro-universe, ad infinitum. While it is not too difficult for us to imagine the concept of infinity as a mathematical construct of this sort, as a number can always be doubled or halved however big or small it may be, the same can not be said for a chain of universes that are constructed from what in our experience seems "actual solid matter".

Since the discovery of the atom, children, writers, and even scientists, have all fantasised about the strange possibilities that this idea conjures, but it has, thus far, always been dismissed as unworkable. The reason for this dismissal is a seemingly-inescapable problem; the logical extrapolation of the concept to the point of infinity would require that the things that we can touch, taste and feel would not actually be made of anything solid at all!

In our world of apparent tangible reality, the idea that matter is not a physical thing seems preposterous, but here is the surprise; weird and wonderful theoretical non-universes of the sort suggested can actually be constructed, albeit in the extra-ordinary world of mathematical formulae. But could such macro-micro universes, constructed from purely non-physical matter, actually be the stuff of which our own universe is constructed?

Whilst it is abundantly obvious that the atom is not an exact miniature of a solar system, the underlying principle behind this concept does lead one to wonder just what such a cosmos of strange and parallel constructs, which fit together like a never-ending set of Russian dolls, could possibly be made from, if not from some kind of particle of matter, however small. The scientists of today struggle to find evidence of the alleged smallest particle, dubbed the 'Higgs Boson' after scientist Peter Higgs, from which, presumably, all matter must be made. We are now forced to ponder just how small the smallest particle might actually be, and equally whether the rules of the theoretical, mathematical multiverse proposed here could apply to our notion of the universe we inhabit and perceive.

Our universe is mostly space, and the distances between its heavenly bodies are relatively gigantic. Therefore, if we were able to compress our universe to its smallest possible size, by removing all the gaps between all the heavenly bodies, our universe would be much, much, much, much smaller. Even so, this would still be a very long way from the infinitely-small size of a fully-compressed mathematical universe. So, could our universe be compressed still further?

Let us consider the case of a small galaxy of 100 billion stars, just to get things into perspective. Even if all the empty space in that galaxy were to be removed, its resultant size would still be relatively huge, from our perspective, with a diameter that was perhaps millions of times greater than the diameter of the largest single star. When we remember that our universe has been estimated to hold about 100 billion of these galaxies, it becomes abundantly apparent that, although our universe would be billions of times smaller if all of the space was removed, it would still be an inconceivably large thing.

But we must remember that, just like the solar systems of the universe, the atoms that make up our universe also consist mostly of space. So what would happen if we first took away all the space between every atom, and within every atom, and then compressed the universe to its smallest possible size? This time we would get a very different result. Our entire universe would be rendered down to the size of a regular football! That our unimaginably large universe could actually be constructed from such a small amount of real solid matter, spread so incredibly thinly throughout such a vastly enormous space, may seem preposterous, but that is precisely the case.

Now consider this. If the electrons and nuclei that make up the countless trillions of atoms of our universe are, in their turn, constructed in the same way, from even smaller particles with spaces in-between, compressing the universe to its smallest possible size would now mean that the football would be so reduced in size that we would not be able to see it, even with the most powerful of electron microscopes. Therefore, extrapolating the concept of construction modes that we know to apply to both the universe and to atoms to just one more sub-atomic stage means that everything in the universe could fit into a space so small that we would not even be able to detect it. Now the idea of a contracting dimensional counterpart, the right hand of our universe in the D4=R view, suddenly begins to seem a far more realistic idea.

But why stop there? If such a process could continue ad infinitum, as mathematics currently attests, should we not consider the possibility that the smallest particle that we currently strive to identify, the Higgs Boson, is in turn made from some other unimaginably small particle? What, then, is matter? Is it some kind of elusive construct derived entirely from unidentified energy fields, oscillating in accordance with a mysterious mathematical code, a code to which the Ancients sought to become attuned so long ago?

As we peer ever deeper, outwardly in search of the limits of the cosmos and inwardly in search of increasingly-smaller particles, a truly bizarre picture begins to emerge. Ultimately, it seems, all the particles that we consider to be physical might not actually be constructed from anything physical after all. Everything that we can see, hear and feel might be conjured by some strange and mystifying marriage of mathematics and energy, the ultimate yin and yang of the cosmos that we have found honoured in the circles and triangles of Stonehenge.

If this hypothesis now seems viable it must be considered that such a yin-yang marriage of forces and formulae might be responsible for the manifestation of the complete physical universe, from entirely non-physical origins. Nothing, therefore, would exist in the sense that we currently consider it to do. All the physical universes, with their many elements, from here to eternity, and the magic that enables life itself to flow throughout the spaces within, might all reside within an unimaginably small, unimaginably great, multidimensional energy field. If, like the universal yang, the yin also has a period of maturation that leads up to the Fertile Age, it might be supposed that it, too, is composed of, or facilitated through, a further eight 'energetic' dimensions.

So the idea of a purely non-physical universal element, as an eight-dimensional energetic construct that we experience rather than touch, does appear to have a place in the developing scientific hypothesis. If this is the yin partner to the physical yang, we now have sixteen of the twenty-four non-time dimensions accounted for. But the geometric representations of the Ancient Celts, the theorems of Ramanujan, and the ideas of the quantum physicists all demand the existence of a further eight dimensions, and so we must conclude that, in order to maintain symmetry, the universe has a third, currently undefined, eight-dimensional element.

141

In order to give some substance to the concept of a triune universe, which has a yin, a yang and (let us now say) a 'yun', we will once again take a leaf from our book of inspiration by reducing the picture to its simplest of elements, and applying some rudimentary logic.

The Ethereal Jewel

In recognising that the signposts of synchronicity are directing us toward acceptance of the concept of a triune universe, we are immediately confronted by another inescapable question; what is the function of the mysterious third element of the universe that has here been christened 'yun'?

The Tome of Seus divides the universe into two aspects or realms by means of the concepts of physical and non-physical elements. This dualistic overview is then utilised to convey the idea that things that cannot be seen or touched can and do exist. However, despite the simplification, the non-physical part of the universe is considered as performing two separate functions, the first of which applies to the concept of the energetic universe. Initially, we are directed to consider the nature of the physical universe, with its mountains, its sky and its seas. These things, we are informed, can be fully described by the laws of the physical universe, whereas the plants, the trees and the animals cannot. In 5:6:21 we learn that:

> Each blade of grass holds something precious that elevates it beyond the laws of the physical. A pure, eternal and unyielding energy that we cannot touch.

This is a clear reference to the soul of mortal life and, as its home must lie outside the physical universe, we can therefore determine that the universe has at least one other, non-physical, 'element' within which this mortal soul resides. In view of our limited understanding of the energetic universe, it is perfectly rational to conclude that its eight dimensions might serve the needs of this 'soul of mortal life', and, from our naïve position, it would seem logical

142

that this essential force of life could indeed be accommodated within the energetic yin. So now we have a dualistic model that can, theoretically, support the body and the soul within its two eight-dimensional yin and yang elements. Why, then, the need for yet another eight-dimensional entity? Why can't symmetry simply be found in the numbers 8 and 16? Why must the non-time dimensions always add up to 8 and 24?

To begin to visualise a non-mathematical answer to this puzzling mystery we must first reconsider the life of the yin-yang universe with which we are now familiar. In the Stonehenge model already considered, the energetic yin and the physical yang came together at the dawning of the Fertile Age, when they had each reached the necessary degrees of energetic and physical maturity to support life. Could we assume that this dualistic universe was capable of supporting the essence of life from the very outset? That life in some form or other could survive the absolute energetic and physical chaos of the Big Bang? Despite the answer to this irksome question being an obvious and emphatic NO, once again *The Tome of Seus* manages to enlighten us with its wisdom in this regard.

> Then we must assume, during that early time, before the universe entered the fertile age, the essence of life must have lain safe somewhere.

And that somewhere, we are assured, is the Ethereal Jewel. This, then, is the third eight-dimensional entity, the mysterious 'yun' element of the triune universe, which serves to support not the mortal soul of our present human condition, but the collective eternal soul of life itself. When the physical and energetic worlds are in chaos, or when these components of the universe are no more, and the ten dimensions rule alone, life must return to the Ethereal Jewel.

In the universal representation at Stonehenge, it is similarly implied that the seed of life entered the yin-yang universe from outside, acknowledging that the spark of life must have existed somewhere

143

else, at least in the early stages, when the dualistic universe we have earlier described would have been incapable of supporting any form of mortal life whatsoever.

While the newly revealed yun element suitably embraces the theological concept of heaven, equally it provides the philosophical bones and the mathematical muscles upon which the physicists might finally begin to visualise the skin of their own beautiful universe.

But, of course, this grand new view is based on the surmised existence of a host of as-yet-unidentified physical and non-physical dimensions. In truth, there may not actually be a continually contracting super dense anti-half of the physical universe. Equally, the somewhat demystified energetic yin partner of the physical universe may actually amount to nothing more than an interesting idea, (although there is much evidence to demonstrate that it exists) and the universe may not be composed of entirely non-physical matter. However, one crucial concept that *The Tome of Seus* has directed us to consider appears to be based in a sure truth. Somewhere, beyond the yin-yang universe that we all reside in, lies a multi-dimensional entity within which the spark of life can dwell in safety in its most essential form, even during periods of extreme chaos in the physical universe. That entity now has a considered, essential and rational purpose, and an appropriately descriptive name. That entity is The Ethereal Jewel.

The Third Quest

Reading:

The Lost Wisdom

Preseli Consciousness is distinguishable from other disciplines of thought by its unusually extreme approach to the development of knowledge. While its wisdoms have clearly been assembled by a long process of great deliberation, they function like a flotilla of conceptual buoys, joined together to create a raft of rationally-deduced, attainable ideals that journey unfettered across a sea of anti-dogma. This progressive philosophy is to be found reflected in the relics of Stonehenge, as, despite their size, the stones were taken down and repositioned as the existing wisdom developed further. In consequence, the holistic form of this philosophy is fashioned by an elegant skin of infinite flexibility, and propelled by the bold and unrestrained hand of liberty. Yet, perhaps most importantly for us, its vision extends to the limits of time and beyond. For a book such as this, which attempts to reconstruct the last plateau of so broad an ancient wisdom, the pages are surprisingly few in number, but this is more a strength than a weakness. As the many gauntlets that are thus scattered will hopefully soon be raised in unison, the city of idealism that so many of us are endeavouring to construct will find its supreme position on the perfected plateau of wisdom that results. The secrets of success, then, are to maintain the rafts well, jettison them if they fail us, and, above all, to keep those that prove worthy firmly tied together.

In this final chapter the primary focus will swing away from the quest to understand how the universe functions, and towards the question of where it is going, and, as part of this process, the stones of Stonehenge will be rearranged yet another time.

Reconstructing the Universe

No longer do we see the universe as simply yin and yang. Accordingly, it is, at last, the time to define the nature of the three elements of the universe more clearly, and in a way that is relevant to the times in which we live. The three eight-dimensional elements are:

> The Physical Universe - with which the physicists are primarily concerned

> The Energetic Universe - known mainly to those who study metaphysics

> The Ethereal Jewel - traditionally, the sphere of interest of the theologians

Thus, an underlying structure of three eight-dimensional elements has now been revealed, which, along with the addition of two further dimensions of time, provides us with the necessary twenty-six dimensions with which to define our universe.

146

The Physical Universe, or yang element, is something that we are all familiar with, and, in a general sense, therefore needs no further introduction. In this book, the existence of the yin, or energetic, element of the universe has been deduced through rational philosophical consideration, but this is not the only way that this mysterious dimensional element can be located. The energetic element is already known to thousands of people who have a talent for dowsing, and many others who are particularly sensitive to the lines of energy that cover the earth in a grid-like fashion. We can be sure that the Ancient Celts were not only aware of this element as the philosophical perception expressed in the layout of Stonehenge, but that they had the ability to detect its lines of energy in actual experience, as it was along these lines that they built many of their important monuments.

The Ethereal Jewel has, equally, been identified through the process of philosophical deduction, but, of course, its existence has been proclaimed before by virtually every religion that has ever existed. Even so, its place in the universal scheme, and its relevance to modern quantum theory, are described here, for the first time, in a scientific visualisation that connects the theological concept of 'heaven' with eight most elusive dimensions of the mathematical world. But where is its geometric representation at Stonehenge? While the mathematical proportions of the Preseli Triangle reflect the entire twenty-six dimensions of the triune universe here revealed, only the physical element appears to be represented geometrically. We have also seen that the Aubrey and Sarsen circles of Stonehenge can be viewed as representations of the energetic and physical elements, but, so far, no ethereal element has been recognised here either. So, does the geometric ethereal representation actually exist within the Stonehenge layout, and if not, might we in our age of modern science be able to complete the final picture?

It has been demonstrated that the original outer circle was created to function as a solar calendar, as the Aubrey holes originally held 56 Bluestones, an appropriate number to create a 364-day calendar. This

147

is in contrast to the Sarsen Circle, which uses thirty stones to represent an alternative 360-day calendar. Interestingly, dividing the 56 stones by eight, the number of dimensions of one element of the triune universe, gives us our seven-day week, or the 'Aubrey Week' as we might now call it. Dividing 364 by 13, the number of dimensions of the universe associated with our dimension of time gives us the 28 days of the average lunar month, and so on.

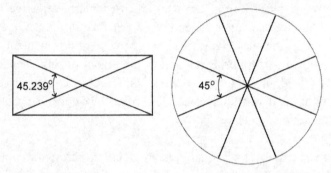

However, the angle that is formed at the crossing point of the two diagonal lines of the Station Stone rectangle is 45.239 degrees, the same angle that forms the point of the Preseli Triangle. Were we to divide the Aubrey Circle (our energetic element) into segments that corresponded to its eight dimensions, the resulting segments (of 1 Aubrey Week) would each possess an angle of 45 degrees at the centre. In consequence, we are forced to consider that this minor discrepancy, a fraction of a degree, might have been considered important to the designers of the monument, particularly as the four station stones were so carefully assigned an identical radius to the Aubrey Circle. It would have been very easy for the builders of the monument to rotate the stone positions slightly, in order to obtain symmetry between the two geometric representations, but it seems that fudging the figures was not their way of doing things. What we discover next is quite possibly a coincidence, but if that is the case it is a truly remarkable one.

For numerical convenience, circles are divided into 360 degrees in our system of measurement. When a circle is taken to be symbolic of a solar year, then, according to the rudimentary rules of mathematics, there must be 360 degree-days in a year, if symmetry is to be achieved. Each of these degree-days is therefore slightly longer than the actual 24-hour periods of light and dark that we think of as days. This is caused by the fact that the actual time it takes earth to rotate about its axis does not fit comfortably with the time it takes to go around the Sun.

Both 360-day and 364-day systems have their merits, and it was presumably for this reason that both were incorporated into the design of Stonehenge. In practice, the calendars at Stonehenge can easily allow for whole day differences with the length of the solar year of 365 days, by periodic realignment. However, if the additional fraction of a day that gives us our familiar leap year had been identified by the Ancients, it would have needed to be accounted for by some other method, for the full solar year to be suitably represented by the circles. The discrepancy between the above mentioned diagonal line angles, of the Station Stones and the Aubrey Circle, is 0.239 degrees, and, lo! and behold, this is precisely equal to the fraction of a degree-day that our modern astronomers tell us the solar year extends beyond the customary 365 days. For those who have an interest in the mathematics, the solar year is 365.242 actual days long, and here are the calculations performed to three decimal places:

(Those who don't like mathematics can look away now):

1 degree day = 365.242/360 = 1.014 actual days

1 degree-day x Discrepancy Angle + 365 = actual days
or:

1.014 x 0.239 + 365 = 365.242 actual days in a Solar Year

The accuracy of the answer is so precise that it actually puts our current Gregorian calendar to shame. In consequence, we might now consider that the Ancients viewed the relationship between the angle

149

of the Station Stone Rectangle and the eight-segmented Aubrey Circle as a unifier of two specific and fundamental harmonies of the universe. The two Pythagorean constituents of this rectangle have already been deduced, in *Chapter One*, as being representative of a unifier of the yin-yang elements of the universe, and later as containing coded references to its twenty-six-dimensional nature.

The Station Stone Rectangle has also long been recognised as a geometric unifier of the cyclical movements of the Sun and the Moon. So it would now seem likely that this rectangle, and likewise the associated Preseli Triangle, were intended to represent the complete universe, where Sun and Moon, male and female, yin and yang all become one with each other. Was this rectangle therefore intended to represent the Ethereal Jewel, the parent of the parents, the ultimate past and the inevitable future?

Before attempting to find an answer to this question, let us take a moment to reflect upon the implications of the discrepancy, conjured by the ingenious integration of the two distinct geometric representations at Stonehenge. The particular harmonic nuance of the number 0.239 is only applicable to the specific cyclic patterns created by the Sun, the Moon and the Earth. As the eyes of our astronomers scour the depths of space for a sister planet, the chance of them finding another that would fit the Stonehenge model as perfectly as ours has to be viewed as being literally billions and billions to one. Nowhere else is there a sun that is orbited once every 365.242 Earth Days, by a planet spinning on its axis once every 24 Earth Hours and bearing a single moon of the same proportions as ours. This not only demonstrates the level of apparent coincidence that is attached to the 0.239-degree discrepancy identified here, but it also reminds us of the strange and wonderful uniqueness of our planet, and, therefore, of its critical importance to the 'Great Scheme' of the universe, should such a great scheme exist.

Unencumbered as we are by the necessity to incorporate a means of measuring the passage of time in our developing geometric representation, the Energetic element of the universe has been symbolised below in its most complete and simple form, that of a circle.

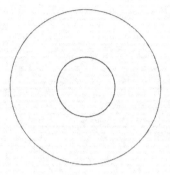

Similarly, the inner circle of the image, derived from the Sarsen Circle, will be used to represent the physical element of the universe in the same way. It has already been ascertained that this circle is also, at times, symbolic of the planet Earth, or the yang father, and this view has been substantiated by the observations of numerous scholars of the past. In his book *New View over Atlantis*, John Michell points out that the outer diameter of the Stonehenge lintel ring is one 200,000th of the polar radius, and that dividing this same radius by 6,000,000 gives us the precise width of the lintels. In his chapter on number and measure he explains the implications of these observations, using distances that have been confirmed by modern satellite surveying systems.

The earth's polar radius, being the shortest distance from its centre to its surface, does not relate to the earth's mean circumference by 2π, but a slightly larger ratio. Comparison of the two measures already obtained for the polar radius and circumference (3949.7142 and 24883.2 miles) shows that the ratio established by the ancients was exactly 10:63. This means that all the principle dimensions of the Stonehenge circle represent simple fractions of the dimensions of the earth.

151

Similarly, therefore, the presumption that the outer circle might also be, at times, representative of the Energetic Earth, or the yin mother, might now be considered to be correct.

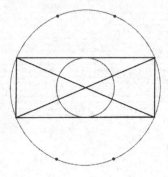

Adding the potentially unifying but previously troublesome Station Stone Rectangle to this picture immediately presents us with a new problem. Unlike the other two circular components, which can be readily divided into eight equal segments, the four Station stones cannot create a symmetrical eight-pointed shape, whichever way they might be connected. To achieve a symmetry that would be appropriate to the representation of the Ethereal element would require the addition of four more points, as represented by the four dots of the above diagram. There is a certain, perhaps intended, irony in the simple observation that, had the builders of the monument provided an additional four Station Stones, suitably spaced around the same perimeter, we would have simply observed an eight-stone circle, and the relevance of the Station Stone Rectangle would never have been perceived in the modern age. It is possible therefore that these points were once indirectly marked, perhaps by stones positioned outside of the core monument, in order to ensure that the solar-lunar connotations of the Station Stone Rectangle would not be missed by future generations.

Now we must introduce another point, to mark the processional entrance at the beginning of the axis of time of the monument. In doing so we discover that we have finally recreated the large Preseli Triangle of Stonehenge, and can label the apex as 't', this point also being representative of our dimension of time. For our modern viewpoint to be complete, it is necessary to add one more point to the diagram that does not appear to have been marked at Stonehenge. Drawing in a point to represent the second dimension of time, -t, renders a second Preseli Triangle within the emerging layout.

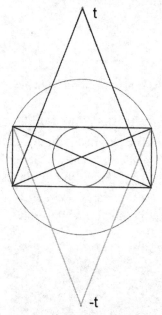

But still our picture is incomplete, as it has insufficient points to be representative of the triune universe. However, reintroducing the four points that we previously discerned were missing from the ethereal representation, and drawing in the respective diagonal lines, also serves to divide the two circles into eight segments each. This brings the total number of segments created by the diagonal lines of the Ethereal element to twenty-four, the magic number of the Preseli Triangle, Ramanujan's mathematical multiverse and the quantum string.

Perhaps more significantly, it also defines the now-symmetrical Station Stone arrangement to reveal at last the hidden geometric symbol of the ethereal element of our philosophically-derived model. And what a surprise we get when we join these points together.

153

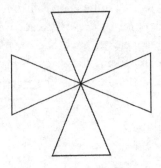

The Ethereal Jewel of the Modern Stonehenge Model

The resulting pattern of the Ethereal Jewel of this modern Stonehenge model, when combined with the circles of the Energetic and Physical representations, reveals a basic symbol that is immediately recognisable as that of the Celtic Cross. The conclusion is inescapable. The Celtic Cross was originally conceived as a geometric representation of the triune universe.

In the interpretation depicted above, the cross is larger than the outer circle, indicating not only that the Ethereal element is all-encompassing but that its radial lines extend outwards, beyond the Physical and Energetic elements, and on to the very periphery of time. This is precisely in accordance with the rational interpretation of the Stonehenge layout that has been revealed here.

A Symbol of Christianity

In its most primitive form the Celtic Cross, or the Jesus Symbol as it is referred to in more easterly locations, is represented by a circle with a cross in it, often with its four segments each subdivided into two sections by a second set of marks or lines.

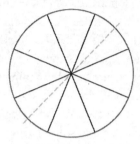

Situated in the Preseli Hills, a little way due north from the circle of Bedd Arthur, lies a marker stone on which one of these symbols was carved, way back in the Neolithic era, thousands of years before the birth of Jesus, and almost certainly in a time before the building of Stonehenge. This seemingly insignificant and humble etching is actually of great historical significance because, drawing in the now familiar invisible line of the axis of time on the appropriate segment of this particular early graphic symbol also marks the precise angle of the Summer Solstice in the Preseli Hills, in exactly the same way that it was later represented at Stonehenge. (At the Preseli Cradle the equinox falls at 49.7 degrees east of north today, a discernible difference of about 1.7 degrees from the 51.4 degrees at the latitude of Stonehenge.)

What we see in this symbol, therefore, is the plan of Stonehenge in its infancy. If Esus is the name we should assign to the father of Preseli Consciousness, the person who conceived the plan for Stonehenge, then perhaps this wheel-like shape should be more properly called the 'Esus symbol', rather than the Jesus Symbol. For this reason, the author has dubbed this stone, which boasts the earliest known representation of this remarkable symbol, 'The Stone

155

of Esus'. After all, it may well have been the product of the father of Preseli Consciousness himself, who, after a day of contemplation, gouged the first proof of his grand design into this humble piece of stone.

So we now have evidence that the Celtic Cross has a history dating back to a time before Stonehenge, and we know from history that it was later adopted by the first Celtic Christians. There is also much evidence to attest that, as Christianity began to spread across the world, the symbol was retained as the accepted emblem of the word of Jesus, before the imposition of the Roman Cross. In those early days, anyone who extolled the virtues of Christianity within the Roman Empire did so at great risk, and being found in possession of the symbol of Jesus by a Roman soldier was likely to result in death. In a highly informative article on the Jesus Symbol, on the pages of *daviddilling.com*, David Dilling reveals that he found examples of the circle at every biblical city he visited on his extensive tour of the Christian world. David also relates how an archaeologist he met in Ephesus, Turkey, enlightened him as to how the early Christians were able to communicate their faith to others without attracting the unwanted attention of the Roman authorities. To do this they used an ingenious encrypted version of the Jesus Symbol, involving the five Greek letters that make up the Greek word for fish:

ΙΧΘΥΣ

The deception was facilitated by the fact that each of the five Greek letters making up the word can be drawn from the lines of the segments of the Jesus Symbol, and, of course, particularly because the word 'fish' is also connected with the biblical Jesus.

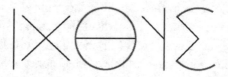

It is due to the Greek penchant for encoding messages into hieroglyphic representations that we realise today that the number 888 was also associated with Jesus in those early times. Now, aware that this same number relates to the numerology of the triune universe of the Ancient Celts, and that the equivalent graphic representation of the concept was also later associated with Jesus, we can only conclude that there was a direct connection between Jesus and the sacred numerology and geometry of the Ancient Celts.

Some three hundred or so years later, the Roman Christians championed the alternative concept of the cross as a mark of the Crucifixion, yet they still honoured the very layout that we have seen at Stonehenge in their design for the *Piazza San Pietro*, St. Peter's Square of the Vatican. However, for some apparently unknown reason, the geometric representation of the Vatican has been compressed in its horizontal plane, towards its central axis, to create an oval rather than a true circle.

The geometry at Stonehenge is very accurately laid out in a true circle, with its proportions reflecting the universal Pythagorean symmetry, and its angular dissections representing various divisions of cyclic time. Even so, comparison with the Vatican layout reveals a remarkable number of precise, proportional coincidences. At many other ancient stone circles the emphasis was placed on symbolic representation, rather than on scientific accuracy, and the circles were elongated along the central axis, this exaggeration no doubt providing a means of specifically symbolising the direction of the axis of time. Bedd Arthur falls on the horizontal axis of time of the Triangle of the Preseli Cradle, and it has its own axis aligned with the Summer Solstice, just like the ancient carving on the marker stone to the north, already referred to, and just like Stonehenge.

Bedd Arthur therefore provides a prime example of an elongated stone circle, and, again like Stonehenge, its outer circle is based on the essential number of eight, in this case subdivided into just sixteen sections in order to perform the rôle of a very simple 364-day calendar. It has been speculated by some that Bedd Arthur was a prototype for Stonehenge, and it certainly has all the ingredients of a 364-day calendar and a ten-dimensional universal representation, complete with a timeline that was originally denoted by two further markers. It would now be rational to consider Bedd Arthur the prototype for *Piazza San Pietro*.

Of particular interest in this history is the observation that, once the emblem had left the shores of Britain, its true and detailed significance was swiftly lost. This is evidenced by the fact that the orientation of the design is wrongly aligned with the cardinal points of the compass in the Non-Celtic variation.

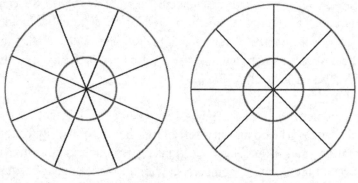

Original Celtic Orientation   Non-Celtic Corruption

In the original Celtic version the vertical axis was aligned to the invisible axis of time, which at Stonehenge was rotated to coincide with the Summer Solstice. The purveyors of the later non-Celtic variation viewed the design purely as an emblem of Christianity, and, unaware of the symbolism of the sacred geometry, they made the now obvious and understandable mistake of assuming that one of the lines of the symbol should be aligned to the 'vertical' north-south axis. We might deduce from this observation that, while the Celtic Christians were the inheritors of the Ancient Celtic vision of the triune universe, the Orthodox and later Roman Churches were merely the inheritors of the symbol. That the symbol should have been associated with Jesus in the first instance adds to the growing

158

body of evidence of a connection between the wisdom of the Celts and Christianity, and further support for these observations will be provided in due course.

It is somewhat ironic that the ultimate symbol of Roman barbaric practice, the cross of crucifixion, doused in the blood of the victims of imperialist lust, including the blood of Jesus, should later be used by the very same people to replace the first, true, symbol of Christ. Thus the Roman hierarchy effectively destroyed the last vestiges of the evidence for the meaning of the true symbol, ensuring that the keys to the origins of the philosophy of Jesus would be lost even to his own sincere followers, and that the Romans' own misrepresentative and over-political interpretation of Christianity would ultimately prevail.

There is a case to be made for the view that the sacred geometry of Stonehenge was exported from Britain before the Christian era, just as its standard units of measurement were. One of several examples that can be raised in support of this argument is the similarity that exists between the layout of Stonehenge and the design of the 'Dharma Wheel' of the Buddha.

It is a generally held belief that the concept of the Dharma Wheel was inherited from the Hindu ever-turning wheel of life, the 'Samsara Wheel', which, like Stonehenge, is also a universal geometric symbol. However, the Samsara Wheel is six-segmented and, from a purely visual perspective, the distinct lack of symmetry shows that this emblem has very little in common with the Dharma Wheel. In contrast, the eight segments of the Dharma Wheel bear a visual similarity to the Celtic Cross so striking that the uninitiated viewer could be forgiven for thinking that one was actually a variation of the other. Its eight radial spokes also extend beyond the limits of the outer circle, exactly as they do with the Celtic Cross. But are these similarities purely coincidental, or was the design of the Buddhist symbol influenced by the layout of the earlier Celtic universal symbol? While it is not possible to derive a categorical answer to this question from a simple visual comparison, the somewhat more critical test of a comparison of geometric proportions will obviously help in assessing the possibility of coincidence. Dropping a representation of the Station Stone rectangle over the Dharma wheel reveals not only that it shares the same specific layout as Stonehenge but that its elements also share precisely the same proportions. That this should be coincidence is extremely unlikely.

The Dharma Symbol conforms precisely to the Stonehenge proportions

Introducing Time

The twenty-four-dimensional universe of the Celtic Cross, represented by the eight segments of the three elements, can only be viewed as fully complete when the two additional dimensions of time are introduced.

The two points at the tips of the Preseli Triangles represent the two dimensions of time, and at both of these points t = 0. So, the centre line of our final plan is like a map of the circumference of the great clock of time, rolled out for us to gaze at in wonder, for here the points t and -t represent both the instant of the beginning and the instant of the end of the universe.

160

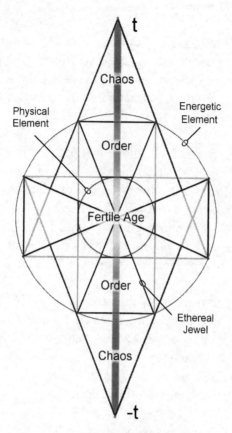

A final geometric representation of the
ten and twenty-six dimensional universe

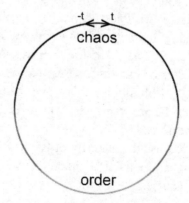

An alternative graphic representation of
time in the cycle of the universe

161

At the instant of the beginning, each hand would have left the zero hour, one travelling clockwise and the other travelling anticlockwise, and, as the moment of absolute chaos was passed, the Big Bang was over and the journey of the formation of the universe would have begun.

The passage of the hand of time in our half of the universe is like the passage of the shaman at Stonehenge. As time progressed it would have journeyed downward through an era of lessening chaos, and eventually crossed the threshold of the age of order. As time continued onward, the seemingly ever-organising universe, now blessed with a stable force of gravity, would have eventually entered its Fertile Age, and, soon after, the journey of life would have begun.

So now we see that there is an all-encompassing great outer circle, described by the two dimensions of time, the perimeter of which symbolises the periphery of the Age of Chaos. We now see also that the circle of the Energetic element can also be viewed as representing the threshold of the Age of Order, and that the inner circle is similarly also symbolic of the Fertile Age.

We are living in this age, at a point which, in this context, is perhaps a little less than half-way through the life of the universe. When time finally reaches the midpoint of its journey, the centre of the great circle of the universe, it will meet its partner once again, and in the instant of their passing, the physical universe will have achieved its most nearly perfect state. Just as the life plan of a mortal being is set to pass through the age of its prime, so the universe will eventually pass beyond its stage of blissful harmony, and the inevitable process of decay will finally begin. It may be worth remembering, at this point, that the universe can in fact never achieve absolute physical perfection, if only because the butterfly of life has flapped its wings. While destiny might choose the destination for the journey, it will be chance that sets the course.

Did the Shamans of old look beyond the glorious days of harmony, the prime of the universe, to see a vision beyond of its ultimate collapse? The presence of four rather than two Station Stones suggests that they did, and this raises the possibility that the point of '-t' might, at one time, have actually been marked at Stonehenge.

In the 1924 title *Stones of Stonehenge* E. Herbert Stone quotes William Judd who, in 1893, wrote about the remains of a mysterious outlying stone.

> Continuing the circuit of the vallum, at the south-west, the visitor will pass over the spot where once stood a stone, which, it is said, marked the setting of the sun at the winter solstice (December 21st). This will be best described by Mr. Dawes, of Bournmouth, which appeared in the January number of *The Astrologer*, 1890.
>
> *[The quotation given is as follows:–]*
>
> "On writing to Mr. Judd, asking him to kindly search in the south-west, he did so, and informed me that he had found the base of a stone; and in a letter to me he says:– 'I find that the base is still in the earth, about a foot under the surface, and is situate about 51 degrees west of south.' "
> (*Stonehenge, pp.* 11-12.)

The position on the 'vallum', at this angle, places this now lost stone precisely on 'Divine Point A' of the second Preseli Triangle of our diagram, further substantiating the case that, at one time, the point 'minus t' of the triangle would also have been commemorated, perhaps by two stones, as it is at the point 't'.

Despite the loss of many of the outlying stones, and subsequent landscaping of the outer areas, it is possible that the archaeologists might still one day unearth the foundations of this symbolic reference point. However, it is also possible that the vision of the

163

future that we are seeking here is already waiting to be found, within the completed picture of the universe that has been gradually materialising before us.

Completing the Picture

The geometric representation of the universe (Page 161) provides us with a basic interpretation of the distant past, and, finally, the opportunity to peer tentatively into the future. In the beginning was the Ethereal Jewel, within which a plan of the essential twenty-six-dimensional, triune universe was held captive, in a magically encoded symphony of numbers. As the plan began to unfold, the energetic and physical elements gradually assumed a favourable order, and, emerging in maturity, entered an inevitable marriage of yin and yang.

We have previously determined that the universal soul must have resided in the safety of the Ethereal Jewel. From this numerical haven the seed of mortal life was passed into the Energetic yin, to be nurtured. From this same non-physical origin came the blueprint for the manifestation of a physical universe, the Physical yang that finally crystallised the necessities of the mortal body. But how, we might ask, could the essential spark of life be transferred between these two wholly incompatible, opposite constructs?

In the simplest of analogies we might recall that the numbers on the magnetic strips of the bank cards that we so frequently rely upon today are placed there by a moving electromagnetic field. Here is a perfect example of data being transferred energetically and received and stored in a physical structure. So the mystery of the transference mode of the DNA code from the Ethereal Jewel to the Energetic Yin, would perhaps have been dependent upon the presence of the Physical Yang. The principle in this analogy, at least, is not so mysterious after all. Mortal life could not possibly have become manifest in the universe until the marriage had taken place and the Fertile Age had begun.

164

But our diagram tells us that, as the hands of time continue on their journey, the Fertile Age will come to an end. Mortal life will therefore become extinct in the universe as the energetic and physical elements begin to merge in chaos, before finally disappearing back into the Ethereal Jewel.

In recent times scientists have considered the possibility that the physical universe (or our five-dimensional half at least) will eventually cease expanding and begin to contract. However, extrapolating the view of the universe as a construct of energy and numbers raises the possibility that the apparent physical manifestation of our universe will simply disappear as the energy runs out, because matter doesn't actually exist in a physical sense. This is the future that is forecast by the geometric model that we have unearthed here. A future in which time essentially returns to its starting point and, perhaps like the seasons of the solar year, the universal year will begin again.

If the foundations of the one missing stone of the Preseli Triangles of Stonehenge were to be rediscovered, we would have absolute evidence that the builders of the monument had constructed a device that could be used to predict the demise of the universe. However, rather than awaiting the conclusions of future possible excavations for affirmation, we might instead look elsewhere for evidence that this was their intention. If the Druids did indeed cast their eyes towards the end of the universe, and, as has been surmised, they also introduced the young Jesus to their philosophies, then evidence of this view may well exist, preserved within the record of the Christian notion of Salvation.

Salvation

Now we are faced with the most difficult of philosophical questions, why was life created, if only to be destroyed? This question is raised in *The Tome of Seus*, with regard to the inevitable demise of the stars, when the protagonist is asked; "if this is the eventual fate of all the suns of the universe, what is the point of our struggle?" The answer that we receive is as simple as it is rational, but rather than being complete, it leads us towards deeper considerations. "If we are to survive beyond the fertile stage, we must transcend our mortal state."

Inevitably, as *The Tome of Seus* reminds us, if we fail in the quest to locate the keys to our salvation, all signs of humanity will be cast into the cauldron of the cosmos, to suffer the same inevitable fate that awaits our entire yin-yang universe. Salvation is a topic that commands an important place in Christianity, and it is therefore worthy of further investigation. The Christ connection has been repeatedly seen, popping up most notably in the 888 structure of the inner Preseli Triangle, in the parallels between the philosophies of the Celts and the Gnostics, and equally in the symbolic geometry and numerology of the Celtic Cross. Further evidence of a distinct association between these two wisdoms can be found in *The New Testament*. In *The Second Epistle General of Peter* 3:12-13 we find a description of the end days of the universe that is highly compatible with the vision revealed here.

> 10 But the day of the Lord will come as a thief in the night; in the which the heavens shall pass away with a great noise, and the elements shall melt with fervent heat, the earth also and the works that are therein shall be burned up. 11 Seeing then that all these things shall be dissolved, what manner of persons ought ye to be in all holy conversation and godliness, 12 Looking for and hasting unto the coming of the day of God, wherein the heavens being on fire shall be dissolved, and the elements shall melt with fervent heat? 13 Nevertheless we, according to his promise, look for new heavens and a new earth, wherein dwelleth righteousness.

In this view we see that, as new heavens and a new earth will be formed, the universal cycle will be repeated. The day when all that exists will dissolve is also now a familiar concept, and the fact that this is the "day of God", at least according to Peter, is of particular interest. Despite his forward-looking vision, Peter is clearly clinging to the notion of the Hebrew scriptures of a paternal God, but when all is dissolved what remains must be God alone, neither paternal nor maternal, neither yin nor yang, neither energetic nor physical. In accordance with the determinations made here, therefore, God, if God exists, must reside within the Ethereal Jewel, and it is to the Ethereal Jewel that the yin and the yang will inevitably return.

Although we must assume that the vision of Peter was based on the philosophy of Jesus, we learn from *Saying 22* of *The Gospel of Thomas* that Jesus viewed the "Kingdom of Heaven" as being neither Paternal nor Maternal, and, presumably therefore, he would also have perceived God in this way.

> Jesus said to them: "When you make the two one, and when you make the male and the female one, so that the male is no longer male and the female no longer female, then you will enter the kingdom".

The obvious implication of this Gnostic lesson is that the ultimate goal can be achieved by seeing beyond the outward differences of the body and of the psychological characteristics of gender. Perhaps Jesus and Mary, having achieved a unification of spirit and attained a high state of consciousness, became the embodiment of mortal perfection and were therefore ready for ascension. This is certainly a philosophical viewpoint that would be more at home in Eastern culture than in the rigidly orthodox teachings of the Judaism of biblical Palestine. On the more holistic level under consideration here, it seems that Jesus may have been providing us with one of the keys to our own salvation. As the yin and the yang dissolve together, they re-enter the Ethereal Jewel. For us, however, the end of the journey must come before the end of the universe. Logically, therefore, we, too, must aspire to make the male and the female one, before the end of the Fertile Age, if we are to return the essence of

167

life to the safety of the Ethereal Jewel. This, then, may be the 'salvation' to which Jesus so often referred.

We are reminded here of the conclusion of *Chapter One*, that the Preseli Triangle symbolises the union of the Sun and the Moon, transcending the yin-yang requirements of the mortal being and accepting the existence of a pure and all-encompassing intelligence. So now we must ask; what is God?

The Ethereal Jewel of philosophical physics can now be viewed as encompassing the theosophical Christian concept of heaven, except that, here, God is not a man or woman, but an eight-dimensional spiritual entity from which time, energy and matter can all become manifest. In this sense, then, God did indeed create the universe, in its now-perceivable yin-and-yang format, but, at this instant, it seems more appropriate to say that the universe was created from God, rather than that it was created by God. Here, in this jewel-like heaven in which the true, as yet undefined, God sits, the force of life can reside in perfect safety when the male and the female cease to exist separately, and merge into wholeness.

This analysis of the similarities between these Celtic and Christian wisdoms directs us to consider the probability that quintessential Christianity originated from a philosophy that had its feet firmly planted in the concepts portrayed in the layout of Stonehenge. Equally, the differences of emphasis between the two disciplines lead us to conclude that the theology of Constantine might have simply misunderstood, or, more likely, misappropriated the philosophies it inherited from the Celts. Reconciling these concepts with the popular paternal view of theology, and then wiping all evidence of the original wisdom from the record, would certainly have facilitated the creation of a new power base, built on a dogma that was perfectly fashioned to ride the flooding tide of the early Christian era. This is exactly what happened at the beginning of the Fourth Century CE, but was it by innocent coincidence, or was it by devious design? Most religious historians would argue that the rise of Roman Christianity was the result of a calculated and well-understood imperialist policy, and this is certainly the view expressed within *The Tome of Seus*. In *Chapter 4*, 4:5:14 we read:

"who is this man who sits in the clouds stroking his beard, despatching mortal messengers to trade eternal life for blind faith? This is not the Duw that I recognise."

As the book uses the Welsh word for God, 'Duw', it is abundantly apparent that this particular encrypted interpretation of Preseli Consciousness does not accept the Roman Christian perception of God; the divine human-like creator of a flawed dogmatic theology that must be followed to the letter for fear of eternal suffering. Later, in *Chapter 6*, the book reminds us that, of course, it was man who created this particular God in his own image.

In *Chapter 5,* the idea raised here, that any 'real God' must exist within the Ethereal Jewel, is corroborated, and we are further reminded that this God is life, and therefore that God resides within all living things, even a blade of grass. It wasn't until the 9th Century CE, when an Indian Guru named Adi Shankara formulated the Advaita, that this non-dualistic position, of the human soul and God being one in substance, was to make its debut in recorded history. In the philosophy under consideration here, this concept is logically extended to include all life.

So now we have forecast a scenario in which neither the God of Rome, nor any of the other paternal Gods of humanity will be there to save us in the end days, yet the vital task of forging the keys for the ultimate liberation of life on this planet is almost certainly a goal that lies beyond the grasp of humanity. In consequence, all hope for the future currently appears to lie in the predictably advanced capabilities of the future offspring of Humanity, perhaps the Mildren whose approach is heralded here. Our most immediate task, therefore, must be to maintain a worthy inheritance for these offspring if we wish to facilitate our own salvation. The longevity of

169

the ancient Celtic society suggests that the rediscovery and implementation of a new social philosophy, based on their proven model, would be beneficial to this quest. However, in order to avoid the potentially destructive influences of another Romanesque interjection, such a vision would need to be rolled out on a global scale. Let us now see if we can add some structure to that old, elusive model.

The Lost Social Archetype

Stonehenge took 1500 years to complete, and each phase of construction would have required the labour of a well-organised workforce of considerable size. Those people who were charged with the task of overseeing the materialisation of the vision would also have needed to ensure that the workforce had somewhere to sleep, and people to feed them. All in all, the construction workers and their immediate supporters would have constituted a large community for its time, and one that would have had the same requirement for housing and communal buildings that any sizable, permanent community would be associated with.

Unlike a conventional township, this community would have been predominantly focussed on the task in hand, the creation of the monument, and in consequence would have required the strong, reliable support of the greater community, particularly for food, tools and clothing production. The provision of raw materials would also have required significant logistical connections to be maintained with outlying quarry teams, which were situated some distance away. That such a long-term project was conceived and successfully executed implies that the supporting community were both affluent and highly developed, with a huge area of South West Britain falling under the influence of a single and highly stable political system. Bearing in mind that similar projects were being carried out all over Britain during this period, it is feasible to consider that the majority of Britain might have been secularly, as well as spiritually, united at this time.

170

The prime products of the age were the enduring monuments, many of which still stand today, thus ensuring that the encoded wisdom could be passed on to generations yet to come, thousands of years after the passing of the civilisation that built them. Stonehenge and the other great monuments of the era were clearly of huge importance to the psyche of a united nation of the time. In our own wasteful age, where we in the West produce utilitarian buildings that are sometimes taken down without ever having have been occupied, we could learn much from the forward-looking, socially responsible, holistic ethos of the ancient world.

In contrast to our buildings, the giant symbols of science and philosophy of the Ancients were conceived within a planning policy that spanned thousands of years, and some of the circles of Britain were actually constructed during the later Bronze Age. Particular to this case is the small circle of Duloe in Cornwall, perhaps erected as a monument to serve the expanding community of the era at the port of Looe, as it exhibits eight stones, the smallest number that can represent the multi-layered vision of Stonehenge. One must now begin to wonder if a belief in the 'three eights' of the wisdom of the Ancients also permeated the long-standing socio-political roots of their society. That these people successfully maintained a harmonious unity, socially, spiritually and, in all probability, politically, for thousands of years, highlights our own great need to rediscover the secrets of their lost social archetype. But where should we look for the forgotten secrets?

We have seen that Blake predicted that the lost wisdom would one day be rediscovered in Britain, and he saw this wisdom as having provided the original foundations for Christianity; hence his belief that 'Jerusalem' would be built again upon those same British foundations. This underlying wisdom was clearly alive in the Bronze Age, up until the time of the Romans, and would therefore have been accessible to Jesus, whose uncle Joseph is recorded as being the overseer of the shipping trade that took Cornish tin to the Turkish bronze foundries. Blake reinvigorated the belief that Jesus and his

171

uncle Joseph once walked upon the green lands of Britain. In *The Almighty King*, long-lost historic evidence to support this claim is re-presented in the form of a solid case for Jesus having been born the son of a British King. As the historical merit of these old beliefs is now finally acquiring due recognition it seems appropriate to consider that something of the lost Druidic ideals might remain hidden within the teachings of Jesus. Therefore, in view of the lack of other written evidence of the Druidic social principles, we will seek to investigate this prospect further by returning to the pages of the gospels for a third and final time.

In *The Almighty King*, the following passage from the *Gospel of Matthew 20:24-28* is quoted as providing evidence that John and James, and Jesus himself, were all subjects of the Gentile hierarchal power system, while the other disciples, not being of royal Gentile blood, were not. This is brought about by the request of the mother of James and John, asking Jesus to find positions for her sons in the kingdom to which he was returning, because they were his blood relatives. While this point is extremely enlightening in itself, the same passage also highlights possible evidence of the alternative power structure that is being sought here. Jesus endeavoured to console the other disciples, who objected to the brothers' attempt to carve themselves positions of privilege on the basis of their family connections, by explaining that there would be a different, independent, and fairer, hierarchal structure in the prospective kingdom.

And when the ten heard it, they were moved with indignation against the two brethren. But Jesus called them unto him, and said, Ye know that the princes of the Gentiles exercise dominion over them, and they that are great exercise authority upon them. But it shall not be so among you: but whosoever will be great among you, let him be your minister; And whosoever will be chief among you, let him be your servant: Even as the Son of man came not to be ministered unto, but to minister, and to give his life a ransom for many.

172

Jesus calmed their concerns by explaining that they who remained were not to be constrained by an inferior, predetermined and archaic system of authority, but that they would be free to choose their own leaders in accordance with an essentially democratic concept. However, unlike its modern political counterpart, this was a system that, he had been at pains to demonstrate, would be forever mindful that a leader should never be too mighty to wash the feet of a follower.

Jesus was advocating a basic concept here, which would be more at home in Druidic or Buddhist society, as superior to the imperfect royal secular system of the Gentiles that had been devised to perpetuate control through inheritance. This highlights a certain contradiction between the secular and spiritual systems of the kings and the Druids, the moguls and Buddhists, which, even so, must have coexisted as the result of time-honoured plateaus of mutual respect. It also demonstrates that Jesus believed that the establishment of a universal social-moral code was something that could be achieved independently of political law, even in the absence of such mutual respect. The history of the first three hundred years of Christianity, within the Roman Empire, serves as certain testimony to the accuracy of that conviction.

This is not the situation that we see today. Politicians steer the democratic world, but while they tolerate religion where it posses an undeniable strength of numbers they afford it nothing in the way of real power. Worse still, they express little or no genuine interest in the salvation of Humanity. One has only to view the recently revealed historic connections between the world leaders and the energy and weapons industries, or to consider the body-count of the needless oil and drug wars, to realise where the loyalties of the world's most powerful and often hidden élite really lie.

Religions tend to view salvation as a soul-by-soul process, as their power is proportional to the size of their congregations. While this is not a bad thing, their messages are effectively confined to the theological stage, and the ever-more-worldly public of the West have begun to turn their heads in droves from the Gods who have failed them. Unfortunately, television, drugs and the dollar seem to have filled the void for far too many.

Perhaps in desperate contrast, *The Tome of Seus* attempts a simple reconstruction of the philosophy of the Druids and their "Lost Social Archetype" on our behalf. Unlike our present system where each discipline maintains a vested interest in its own agenda, and the politicians, the priests and the scientists all have pulpits of their own, the Druids had but one agenda and spoke with a single tongue. Their leaders were the wisest and most intuitive members of their ranks, who formed the 'Circle of the Keepers of Truth' where knowledge was challenged and wisdom was progressed for the benefit of all humanity. They did not proclaim policies that would lead to prosperity, but pursued a truth that would lay a path to the salvation of us all. In their house they would learn the secrets of each and every discipline, in order that they might view their responsibilities, to advise, to educate and to heal, from a totally holistic vantage point. Neither was theirs a prosperous endeavour, as, although they were greatly respected and well patronised, they were also the humble servants of the people. That the monarchy was itself of Druidic persuasion ensured that the King was also perceived as a servant of the people, and peace and prosperity for all was a primary political goal. This vision is very much in keeping with the model presented in Matthew's gospel. However, it was Matthew's conviction that the ultimate rule of the monarchy was to be dissolved in the kingdom of the future, thus demonstrating that the ideal society could be built independently of political influence, and that Druidic truth was ever an evolving goal.

We might now begin to wonder whether this handful of humble principles contains the rudimentary components of a crude but crucial survival plan, which has been slowly unfolding in the hearts of humanity from the very first moment that Stonehenge was

174

conceived. If so, then the time has come for our quest to begin, quietly, and with or without the blessing of political law.

The Quests of Esus

If Blake was a prophet, then this new social quest will finally see the building of his 'Jerusalem' as the Age of Aquarius begins to dawn, but with change comes disruption, and so we must expect that the path that lies ahead will not be smooth. In its turn, disruption brings the need for change, and, if this ever-turning wheel of fortune is to move towards more fruitful pastures, we must learn to steer a righteous course for our final quest. However, according to "The Triple Metaphor" considered in *Chapter 6*, there were three quests, one of the past, one of the present and another of the future. Hence, before considering the third quest in greater detail, we will take a brief look at the earlier quests, which have allegedly laid the foundations for the change that promises to lift us from the ashes of our own wrong-doing.

According to *The Tome of Seus*, the first quest was that of Esus I, who, dissatisfied with the beliefs of the society in which he lived, retired to the woods to contemplate the purpose of life. Eventually Esus emerged with a pragmatic and foolproof approach to salvation that was to grip the imagination of his king and become an established system of belief amongst his soon-to-be-enlightened brethren. Search only for the truth. As each element of Truth is contemplated and agreed, pass it on into the Knowledge. Grant the Knowledge only to those who seek Unity, and as the Knowledge and its community grows, so will the potential for the transcendence of humankind to become manifest, for heaven on earth and earth in heaven to be attained. And so a philosophy was born, based on the pursuit of Truth, Knowledge and Unity, enabled through a marriage of intuitive spirituality and rational deliberation and revealed in a yin-yang perception of the cosmos that is unmistakably one of the keys of the wisdom of Preseli Consciousness.

175

It was this simple philosophy that led the ancient people of Briton to build their deep understanding of the universe, to predict the rise and fall of the tides and to calculate the movements of the sun and the moon. From here they were able to develop mathematical formulae and engineering principles that survive in the measuring systems and calendars of the present day, and which enabled the construction of the great monuments to begin.

Then, as the wheel of fortune turned, the intrusive political philosophy of Rome was formulated and soon after came devastation for the Celtic ways. As the imperialist plot gradually gained momentum, the time was right for the quest of Esus II, 'an exchange of wisdoms' as a preparation for the day when the pursuit of Truth, Knowledge and Unity would be recognised by all as the path to freedom. This is an interpretation of the primary goal of Jesus, which was allegedly intended to extend and share the wisdoms of the Celts with the philosophies of the other world religions. The famously documented three and a half years of his life that were spent in Galilee and Judea certainly inform us that the remaining thirty or so years, lost to the biblical record, must have been spent elsewhere. Jesus was not the property of Rome, and his philosophy was clearly not the product of a solely Judean education. Evidence exists to place him in Britain during his formative years, and in India after his brief return to Jerusalem at the age of twelve. And so, although this may not be the place for such a debate, it must be noted that a basic argument for this claim is not difficult to make in a real historical sense.

The Second Quest, therefore, was to sow the seed for one-great-wisdom, which would eventually spring from the soil of humanity and lead us away from the precipice of destruction. In the end, greed and aggression cannot prevail. The greatest success of the current path would be the ultimate instrument of its own failure, total destruction, but this simple truth has proved to be most difficult to learn. When the systems of the present begin to crumble, the true wisdom will gain the opportunity to rise again, from the dormant

176

seed of its distant past. Let us hope that the seed is nurtured as the day of deliverance approaches.

While our future appears to be determined by our ability to revise our philosophies and modify our social archetypes, in the holistic view of the Ancient Celts science also had a decisive rôle to play. We have seen that the survival of life depends upon the continuity of a favourable environment within the physical and energetic universes, in which the soul can manifest in a mortal state, which is to say in the body. Survival beyond the predictable collapse of that environment will require an understanding of the mechanisms that permit our return to the safe haven of the spirit world, the Ethereal Jewel. Acquisition of this gem of knowledge is therefore the eventual goal of our journey through this universe, as it is the ultimate key to our salvation. As we approach the precipice of premature physical ruin we will realise in the starkest terms that our destiny is very much of our own making. Failure to act responsibly in our duties as caretakers of our physical and spiritual environments will result in catastrophe, as we will arrive at the doors of salvation long before the keys to open it have been successfully forged. Under such circumstances, no matter how we might cry, the doors to eternal life will remain firmly locked. The Third Quest therefore must eventually involve us all, for unless we unite in our efforts to discover another way, the current path towards destruction will prevail.

And so we might deduce that Esus III will not descend through the clouds in a chariot, as a mortal incarnation of God, to save the good and condemn the evil in a final day of judgment. Instead, the third incarnation of Esus, referred to as "the spirit that is yet to be", will manifest within the collective consciousness of humanity, if it is to manifest at all.

The Third Quest of Esus is, therefore, the quest of the Esus that resides within us all, to unite the world in the pursuit of salvation through the re-creation of the 'Circle of the Keepers of Truth'.

177

Whosoever will be great among us, we will let him be our minister, and in this new international circle of elders, the greatest minds of the social, theosophical and scientific disciplines will take their rightful places. Each time they meet they will ask themselves the question, "What is truth now?" and the journey to acquire the keys to salvation will have resumed.

A Brief Conclusion

In the final analysis, the origins of the simple philosophy revealed within this book are of academic interest only, as these origins have no bearing on the purpose of the philosophy. If the philosophy is well read, and deemed worthy, then humanity will progress towards its goal. The various credits for the new discoveries and the rediscoveries of archaeological and scientific significance are, similarly, of historic interest only. If they prove to be correct, then our understanding of our universe will grow, and our prospects for survival will be improved. Esus, Plato and Pythagoras are but names, as royalties cannot be paid to the dead. For this most obvious reason, there is no reason for a philosophy to be bound to a history, or for a truth to be claimed by a nation. Truth is the entitlement of all, regardless of colour, gender, race or creed.

For us, the search for truth is a never-ending quest. Sadly, this simple conviction is impossible for the majority of the world's theologians for they stubbornly cling to what they believe are unchanging and unchangeable truths, handed to them by men of old whose still-echoing voices claim a divine authority which in fact can never be substantiated. Can they all be possessors of the truth? Can they all have had their diverse and often opposing beliefs passed to them by the voice of God? If so, we might wonder why it is that they cannot explain the mechanisms of their own God's universe, and why they have led their people into so many conflicts, rather than into an ever-strengthening union.

For the final thought, it seems appropriate to consider the last words of the book that has provided the inspiration for this work.

> When The Circle is complete and people everywhere join their hearts and souls to step inside, I will be waiting.

As we read the words "I will be waiting", we are reminded of a fundamental wisdom that has underpinned the very fabric of the philosophy revealed here, that "God is life and is within us all."

In this sense, then, the Bible is perfectly correct in its claim that Jesus was the Son of God, as we are all sons and daughters of God, and, collectively, we can and must aspire to become one with God if we are to attain salvation. When this universe is gone, and another develops to the point at which it can once again support life, will we be waiting?

Now we might ask, did DNA have an evolution after all, in a long-lost universe that preceded that of our own? Did intelligent life eventually discover the ultimate secret of survival, by assembling the critical wisdoms that had to be realised if the blueprint of life was to survive beyond the inevitable destruction of each ultimately-forgotten cosmos?

As we slowly unravel the secrets of the magic numbers of this universe we are taking the first deliberate steps to acquire the status of custodians of that very same wisdom. Perhaps our old perception of God relates more to our most distant of ancestral species, which survived long enough and evolved far enough to secure the future of life, by placing the Big Code of antiquity safely into the Ethereal Jewel for us to inherit.

We too can aspire to that goal.

End Notes

The 3D Preseli Triangle

A remarkable Altar Stone, rescued from a pile of rubble that was recovered by Celtworld from the old stonewall of a Pembrokeshire hotel, has turned out to contain an ingenious three-dimensional representation of the Preseli Triangle. It is clear from the weathering of the stone that it was originally fashioned, many thousands of years ago, into a geometric shape of very specific and accurate dimensions, and that these dimensions relate precisely to the movements of the moon and the dimensions of the universe.

Neolithic Bluestone Obelisk ~ Altar Piece

This particular Altar piece was clearly well worked to a very high standard when it was first fashioned many thousands of years ago. Unfortunately the tip of the stone has been broken off in recent times, the weathering of the break being indicative of a time of perhaps one to two hundred years ago, when the hotel garden wall in which it was found was first built. It is actually feasible to consider that the break might have occurred much more recently, as the weathering effects often penetrate right through small areas like the point of this of stone. However, despite the considerable passage of time since the stone was made, and the more recent unfortunate damage, the original shape of the obelisk is still easily discernable and has been reproduced in the diagram below.

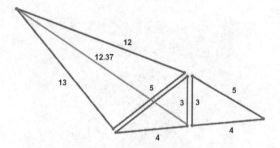

The 3 Dimensional Preseli Triangle viewed from the base

Here we have evidence that the Neolithic people of the Preseli area were not only capable of working stone to a very high degree of accuracy, but that they were able to unify the complex dimensions of the universe and the movements of the moon within a single three dimensional geometric representation. The proportions of the two Pythagorean triangles of the base equate mathematically to the three, eight dimensional elements of the universe, creating the same combination that is reflected by the Celtic Cross and the Christ Number.

$$3 + 5 = 8$$
$$3 + 5 = 8$$
$$4 + 4 = 8$$

The two triangles of the sides represent the left and right hand elements of the universe, with the short and long sides representing the ten and twenty six dimensional time-inclusive interpretations of the universe, and the other two sides representing the total of 24 non-time dimensions of the universe.

For the sceptics, who point out that the 3:2 ratio point of the lunar triangle is not marked within the Station Stone rectangle of Stonehenge, and therefore claim that the Neolithic people were not aware of the advanced mathematics associated with this triangle, peering into the above shape reveals that the inner triangle of this ancient Altar Stone has a short side value of 3. Consequently, the 3:2 ratio point is clearly represented here and the all important hypotenuse of 12.37, the precise number of lunations in a solar year, is perfectly represented by the overall height of the altar piece. Proof, yet again, that the wisdom represented by the Stonehenge layout originated in the Preseli Cradle.

Celtic influences on Egyptian Wisdom

Several studies have uncovered a large number of distinct design similarities between Stonehenge and the Pyramids, and some of their writers have set out to prove that it was the builders of the Pyramids who informed the builders of Stonehenge how things should be done. This is despite the fact that the Celtic monument pre-dates its Egyptian counterpart. Stonehenge I is now known to have been built from Bluestone around 3050 BC, while the oldest building of the Giza Complex, The Great Pyramid, is believed to have been built around 2560 BC, some 500 years after Stonehenge I.

Proof can now be offered here that the Ancient Egyptians also recognised the importance of the appearance of the stone types selected by the Ancient Celts to construct their monuments, and duly honoured these special significances in their own choice of materials for The Great Pyramid. The stones chosen for the bulk of the building were local sandstone and rough sandy-limestone, of very similar appearance to the Sarsen Stone used to build Avebury and, later, Stonehenge II. This could be coincidental, of course, as, in both cases, these materials were relatively convenient to the sites. On the other hand, the alabaster and limestone floors of The Great Pyramid, and many of its casing blocks, are very similar in appearance to the chalk floor of Stonehenge, and these were ferried in a vast effort involving specially constructed ships. Both this material and the construction method itself also compare very closely with those of the Silbury Hill chalk 'Pyramid', which it may be pertinent to note is of similar size to the smaller Pyramids of Giza.

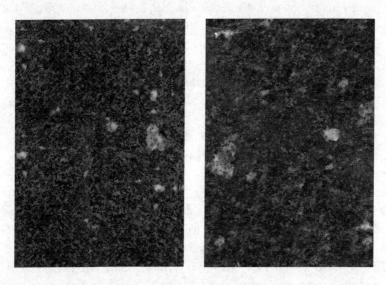

Spotted Dolerite of Stonehenge and Spotted Diorite of The Great Pyramid

The other two stones of particularly notable appearance that were used in large-scale British Neolithic monuments are Bluestone and Shapstone. The striking night sky pattern of the Bluestone (spotted dolerite) seems to have impressed its prehistoric first users as representing, at that unique location of Carn Meini, the entire Cosmos that slowly circled around and over them each night. In view of the interpretation of the Stonehenge layout that has been revealed here, this observation, first published by this author in 2000, seems now even more likely to be correct. It might therefore be considered less than coincidental that the stone chosen for the ornate entrances of the great chambers of the Pharaohs is the one stone of Egypt that bears a conspicuous resemblance to the Bluestone. This stone, spotted diorite, was shipped along the Nile all the way from Aswan in the Deep South and lavished with millions of hours of attention by the most accomplished masons in the world of that time.

Rose Granite of Shap and Rose Granite of The Great Pyramid

Shapstone, the other 'special stone' of the Ancient Celts, was used to construct a huge megalithic complex that once stood in modern-day Cumbria, a monument that would rival Avebury in scale had it not been destroyed to make way for a railway. Shapstone is a particularly attractive rose granite, and is virtually indistinguishable from the rose granite of the Pyramids, which was carried on a nine-hundred-kilometre journey from the quarries of the south and used to adorn the walls and floors of the 'Kings and Queens' chambers.

The conclusion here must surely be that, in a visual sense, the Egyptians embraced the Celtic principles of universal representation when they subsequently constructed the more elaborate complex at Giza.

The Symbol of "The Tome of Seus"

This symbol, found in the original Celtic Wheel, the layout of Stonehenge, The Dharma Wheel of Buddha and the Celtic Cross of Jesus, is used to represent the Circle of the Keepers of Truth.

Time Within Time

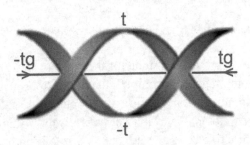

Further to the discussion on time, (*Chapter 8: Introducing Time*) the circular graphic representation of the cycle of the universe becomes a double helix when it is plotted against the timeline of the Greater Universe.

Bibliography

Anon – *The Tome of Seus* – thirdquest.org, 2010, (originally published on 08. 08. 08.)

Blake, William – *The Notebook of William Blake* – unpublished, 1787-1817 (Original work currently held by The British Library)

Bruce, F. F. – *The Gospel of Thomas, Faith and Thought* – The Victoria Institute, 1961

Bushell, William Done – *Caldey, An Island of the Saints* – Lewis Printers, Carmarthen, 1968

Clark, Neil A. – *Stonehenge Bluestone II: The Story of the Secret Preseli Treasure* – Celtworld.co.uk, 2011

Dilling, David – *The Origins of the Christian Fish Symbol* – http://www.daviddilling.com/Christian-fish-symbol-of-Jesus.htm, February 2012

Einstein, Albert – *Relativity The Special and General Theory* – Three Rivers Press, 1952

Farrah, Robert W. E. – *The Megalithic Astronomy of Lundy: Evidence for the Remains of a Solar Calendar* (*Lundy Field Society Annual Report, 1992, No 42*)

Farrah, Robert W. E. – *Symbolic Alignment of St Helena's Church* (*Lundy Field Society Annual Report, 1992, No 43*)

Isenberg, Wesley W. (translator) – *The Gospel of Philip* in *The Nag Hammadi Library* – HarperCollins, 1990

Israpilov M. I. – *The Evolution of Earth Axis Deviation,* in *Holocene // Rhythm Journal, 2, 49-63* – www.rhythmjournal.com, 2008

Johns, Einon – *The Almighty King* – Celtworld.co.uk, 2011

Jones, David – *Footprints in the Stone* – ATP Publishing, 2011

Kaku, Michio – *Hyperspace: A Scientific Odyssey Through Parallel Universes, Time Warps, and the Tenth Dimension* – Doubleday, 1994

King James Translation – *The Holy Bible, Masonic Edition* – Collins, London, 1951

Knight, Peter & Perrott, Toni – *The Wessex Astrum Sacred Geometry in a Mystical Landscape* – Stone Seeker Publishing, 2008

Lewis, E. T. – *Mynachlogddu Pembrokeshire: A guide to its Antiquities* – E. L. Jones & Son, 1967

MacKillop, James – *A Dictionary of Celtic Mythology* – Oxford University Press, 2000

Mac Cana, Proinsias – *Celtic Mythology* – Chancellor Press, 1996

Michell, John – *The New View Over Atlantis* – Thames and Hudson, 1983

National Geographic, *Great Druid Massacre* (Video Documentary) 2008

Parker, Dr. Gary – *Creation Facts of Life* – Master Books, 2009

Patterson, Stephen and Meyer, Marvin (translators) – *The Gospel of Thomas* – www.gnosis.org – 2009

Redman, Patricia – *The Depth of Evil* – Publisher Unknown, 2009

Robinson, J M. (editor) – *The Gospel of Mary* in *The Nag Hammadi Library* – Harper Collins 1990

Stone, E. Herbert – *Stones of Stonehenge* – Robert Scott, 1924

Stukeley, Rev. Dr. W. – *Abury, a Temple of the British Druids* – London, 1743